Paid
The Privilege:

Hearing the Voices
of Autism

By
Dan Reed

©Copyright 1996 Dan Reed

**Paid for the Privilege:
Hearing the Voices of Autism**

Copyright 1996 © **Dan Reed**
All rights reserved. Except for brief excerpts for review or commentary, no portion of this publication may be reproduced without permission of the author.

A *"Movin' On"* book from DRI Press
PO 5202 Madison, WI 53705
Orders and Catalogue Information 1 800 376 0836

DRI Press is a Division of
Developmental Resources, Inc.

Artwork by R. Padre Johnson, Cody, WY
Cover design by Julie Dobson-Miner, Touch of Design, White Bear Lake, MN
Layout Design by Spectra Images, Minneapolis, MN

This book presents the author's personal experiences and beliefs and does not necessarily reflect the views of Midway Training Services, or of any other institutions and individuals referred to in the book. The names of persons in the book have been changed and the persons sometimes represent composites of individuals that the author has observed and interacted with at various agencies and schools.

*This book is dedicated to
the caring, loving people associated
with Midway Training Services.*

Paid For The Privilege

Prologue	1
How Do You Take Your Coffee?	3
And The Name, Again?	13
I'd Rather Have A Root Canal	20
The Pun And The Couch Potato	25
"Screw You"	30
"Please, Call Me Mathew"	34
Don't Turn Out The Lights, The Party Has Just Begun	43
Have Letterboard Will Travel	47
Jack	54
Sam	58
Arnie	63
FC Half-time Update	65
Leona Is Endearing	75
"I Love To Pound On Dem Keys"	78
Welcome Back, Son	84
Padre Knows People	87
Reject The Expected	91
Cruise (Not Bruise) Control	98
You Can See Better If You Get Close	103
The Christmas Gift	109
"Ouija Board" Or Letterboard?	112
Since We Have Your Attention	117
"Dream A Little Dream"	126
Some Final Notes From The Authors	130
"How We Doin', Man?"	133
Epilogue	147
Postscript by Anne Donnellan, PhD	149

Prologue
From a silent voice of Autism

I sit here wondering what it will take for these people to start seeing us for who we are. I am a man who has many qualities and I care about all those around me. Too much thinking with little or no talking or activity is dangerous. And in our world, force seems to speak louder than words. I guess that is why we are in a scary place.

It is hard to explain, but our brains may work somewhat differently from yours. We probably see, hear and even feel things differently from you.

We sit, rarely accomplishing much, and pretty much hide in our own world. It is lonely and wrong. Not many seem to think we know much, but we do and we want to know more. The time is coming when we no longer will have to feel detachment and isolation. We will belong, but we need your help.

Wasting away is not what God has intended for us. A system with many misinformed people feel that enough is being done, and others feel that they have their hands tied by rules and regulations. Ironically, in those very hands lie part of the answer we have all been waiting for. If they give us their hand, we can help guide them to us. In turn, we can help change this place by coming to them. We want to come and all we need is your help.

Finally, someone is coming to us, and we will come to meet him. In the pages that follow you will learn our story. The waiting may be coming to an end, like I said, "all we need is a little help."

Sincerely,

Randy

Chapter One

How Do You Take Your Coffee?

A few years ago if you had asked me if I were going to write a book about my experiences with people diagnosed as autistic, I would have looked at you as if you were autistic.

By profession I am, or I should say, was a business person. I lived, breathed, and succeeded in the business world. I at one time owned my own company, went to power-broker meetings, had lots of important customers, even drove a fancy car. But through a series of what could be construed as unfortunate circumstances, I found myself out of work and in need of a job. An ad appeared in the Sunday classifieds about a Marketing Director job. I sent a resume. And as for the rest, it's in the book.

MARKETING DIRECTOR
ST. PAUL AGENCY

Must be self-motivated. Good with people, strong communication skills. If interested, send resume to:

MTS, 1549 University Ave,
St. Paul, MN 55114

- *Self-motivated? Yes*
- *Good with people? I've been told I am.*
- *Communication skills? Sure, sometimes ad nauseam.*
- *Interested? I don't know. I guess so. A job's a job—and I need a job.*

Can I really deal with another interview? Looking for work gets mighty depressing—the same questions—the same answers. Impress—be impressed, ugh. But if I'm going to be on time, I'd better get moving. Who knows? Maybe this will be the job where I can actually make a difference—help change the world. Yeah, right, but before I start saving the world, I'd better find 1549 University to see what this job is all about.

Driving along University Avenue, I notice several modest but well-kept business places with their holiday lights blinking in the windows. Good! Kind of a neighborhood in transition. The neat window decorations give me a comfortable feeling about the area. Then I drive up to 1549. I groan, "I can't believe it—so shabby—so run-down—so..., oh well, remember, fella, it's what's inside that matters."

The brief building directory just inside the front door points out my destination—Midway Training Services-3rd floor. Proceeding up the steps I have the uncomfortable certainty that this building has been overlooked in the neighborhood-in-transition movement. The stairs are dark and creak at every step. What is left of the original paint on the walls is a nondescript color and peeling in many spots. I begin to wonder who would work here.

Just then, a man bounds down the stairs, hell-bent on escaping the place. But as he speeds toward me, he stops, looks me straight in the eye for a moment, then continues his flight. Just behind him is someone either joining the escape, or trying to retrieve the rebel. This fellow looks as if he has just returned home from a long tour with the Grateful Dead: clothes that have survived the 60's, long hair and a beard, lit ciggy hanging out of his mouth. Huffing and puffing, he asks, "How we doin', man?"

Automatically, I respond, "Groovy." I am quite sure I haven't said "groovy" for 15 years.

At the second level of this building that time and paint have forgotten, I feel another unsettling presence. Several presences, actually. Behind a glass window, I see people milling around. A few of them have seen me; their intensity stops me momentarily. They are not just looking at me; they are interviewing me with their eyes. I move away and continue my expedition up the dark stairway to the 3rd floor. I want this interview over quickly.

At the top of the stairs is a heavy steel door. When I push it open, glaring lights almost blind me. Nothing, not even my greeters on the dark stairway, have prepared me for the noises I hear—the cries, the moans, the sounds of glass shattering. I step back against the door. I struggle unsuccessfully to gain my composure. Is this an office or a Fellini film set? The huge, high-ceilinged room is a maze of cubicles. A noisy cast of characters approach me. Is this my welcoming committee? I feel completely disoriented. What am I doing here?

My query is left unanswered as I am surrounded by the "welcoming committee." My first greeter positions herself two inches from my face and whines, "What is your name?"

I manage to answer, "My name is Dan. What is yours?"

"Gloria. I want to go home."

Gloria, so do I!

My second greeter is much bigger and more threatening in appearance.

This guy can toss me six or seven blocks if he wants to.

"Why are you here?" he demands. Before I can utter a sound, he answers his own question. "We know why you are here."

Gulp.

My final greeter chimes in, "You are going to be our new friend. You must stay."

I spy something that resembles a receptionist desk. I address the woman behind it.

"I am here for an interview."

"You ARE?"

"A-a-a, yes. I have a 10:30 appointment with Barb Kale."

"Hmmm. Here is an application. Take a —"
She stops in mid-sentence, "Oh no—oh God—Earl. No, Earl. Sir, for your own protection, get out of Earl's way. He'll run you down to get to my coffee. Oh God." She moves toward the intercom, "George Bush, George Bush. We have a G.B. situation at the front desk!"

Then I hear the sounds of people running, running from all over the building.

Are they coming here?

Meanwhile someone, *the* Earl, I presume, has gulped down two cups of coffee and has gone for the pot. He now is trying to tip it down his throat.

The sounds materialize as people of various sizes and shapes (including the Grateful Dead guy) run into the room.

What is this? Can I escape? No, now I am surrounded, but at least I am out of Earl's way.

"Get him out of here—he's got coffee all over my desk," the secretary screams.

A small but determined woman brushes the others aside and confronts the culprit, "Earl," she scolds, "If you keep this up, we won't take you to the State Fair."

*The State Fair? The only state fair that I know is in August. This is December—that's quite a wait **not** to get to do something!*

"Clown! Clown!" Earl yells as he points to himself. "Clown! Clown!"

Earl is right—this place is a circus and Earl is in the center ring.

When his performance ends, the semi-composed secretary turns to me and (can you believe it) asks, "Would you care for a cup of coffee?"

I gulp, and choke out, "No thanks."

"Why don't you go into Barb's office and make yourself comfortable? She will be up directly."

Make myself comfortable? Only if there is a bolt on the door.

Since no new incident seems to be *brewing* (I am addicted to puns in times of stress), I follow her suggestion. As I wait, I wonder if I will be calm enough to be coherent. My face is so hot I feel as though I have been attacked by some mysterious fever. With all the turmoil, this interview already qualifies as an out-of-body experience, and I have yet to answer one question.

A few minutes later, an attractive, youngish woman appears. "Hi, I am Barb Kale. I am the Executive Director of Midway Training Services. Did you find us OK?"

"Yes, no problem."

*Locating you, that is; **finding** you **OK**, is quite another.*

In spite of all the obvious chaos, she seems very much in control of herself and her surroundings.

This woman is sharp. Why is she in this place?

"Let me take a minute and explain what goes on around here," she begins.

If she can explain what goes on around here in one minute, she has my vote for any office she wants.

"We are a day center for mentally-disabled adults," she continues, "mentally retarded and autistic adults. Our clients live in group and foster homes, institutions and some live on their own or with their parents. Our mission here is to help get our clients able to work in the community. We serve about a hundred people. We have a staff of 30 which consists of training specialists, behavioral analysts, speech and occupational therapists. And we need a marketing director to help find our participants jobs. That is why you are here now. Why don't you tell me about yourself?"

As I prepare to spout a litany of my vast knowledge of the marketing world, we are joined by a very slim-looking gentleman in his early 30's, casually dressed, but neat right down to his two-foot ponytail. In my many interviews through the years, this is my first ponytail.

"I am sorry to be late, but Sam took out two staff and kicked a hole in the door. Four of our staff got her into the van and are taking her home."

Taking her home? A woman "took out two staff?" If a woman client could accomplish that, what could some of the guys that I met in the hallway do?

"My name is Ray, are you Dan?"

"Uh, yes, I am," I stammer, my mind still on Sam's "Van Ride from Hell." "You say I would find jobs in the community for these people?"

I wonder if Roller Derby is hiring. Would have enough players for our own team here.

Before I can return to my litany about my marketing prowess, Ray jumps in and asked, "How would you deal with conflict?"

Call 911.

But I respond with a more appropriate question of my own: "Could you be more specific about the conflict?"

"Sure, say you have a co-worker who doesn't believe that one of our clients should work in the community and you have an excellent job opportunity, how would you convince the staff that this person should get a chance at the job?"

My mind is spinning. I can see Sam as a bouncer at some biker bar; what a service she would provide to the community. (Not an acceptable answer)

Before I can come up with a reply, I hear someone looking for GEORGE BUSH again, but this time in the alley. Ray jumps up and runs out. "Someone must be trying to run out the back door or something," Barb calmly surmises. "People are sure in a hurry to get out of here."

Makes sense to me.

Ray never returns to the interview; I never get a chance to answer his burning question. Barb and I do talk about marketing strategies and team building, all that management malarkey. Strange as it may seem, I began to like her and to respect what she is attempting to accomplish.

The interview continues for about an hour and a half. Barb says that she is impressed with my answers, but she has many others to interview. I would hear from them within a week or so.

Right. God, I hope that other job comes through.

My attention has already turned to the issue of my safe departure from this place.

Can I escape to the street before I am noticed?

As I move toward the exit sign, I look to see if the coast is clear.

Whew, no more Earl or his buddies.

Suddenly, seemingly out of nowhere, a rather menacing-looking man is in my face. Let's say his comfort zone and mine differ. If I want to, I can count his nose hairs. He looks at me and says, "I know why you are here. We are going to become quite close." I can feel his intensity as he backs away. I too, back away, frantically reaching for the door knob.

The knob is in my hand and I am away. Bounding down the steps, purposely not looking into the second floor window.

Quick! Get the outside door open!

Ten degrees above zero, but nothing cools my still feverish face. As I fumble for my keys to gain the much-needed security of my car, I reassure myself.

They will never give me the job. No one really wants a free-thinker, a strong communicator with good people skills. Sounds good, but these types never get the jobs.

Still in a state of shock, I wonder if Earl is again on the prowl for "unattended" pots of coffee and what does George Bush have to do with Midway Training? What can I do to help these people? From what Barb says, most of them cannot speak or hear, many with the mental age of a two year old, some with paranoia and other mental illnesses. How can I use my much-vaunted communication skills when my clients cannot communicate with me? Impossible.

But try as I might, I cannot not dismiss the eerie communications that have occurred: "I know why you are here." And "You are going to be our friend."

Oh, shrug it off, Dan. They'll never hire you.

Chapter Two

And The Name, Again?

February

Check my tie, one more time.

God, I hate first days! Have to meet everyone, try to remember their names. Nobody remembers *my* name. A lot of "Nice to meet you, Dave—or Don—or ?" No one ever remembers. God, I hate first days.

While walking up the front steps, I think about that comfy sales job in the suburbs that I interviewed for. Nice quiet area, beautiful building, calm, friendly people. But forget it; someone with "more qualifications" got the nod. Now here I am at 1549 University. Quite a contrast. Of all of the many others interviewed for this job, I have to be the *least* qualified. And irony of ironies, I am the one picked. Hired to help autistic adults. Autism. What is autism anyway? Well, it can't be too much of a mystery. I guess I'll soon find out.

Seven forty five, good, I'm early...

As I push the steel door open, I can hear the phone ringing.

"Midway Training, good morning."

That's Barb, she gets to work early, too. She spots me—waves me into her office.

As she hangs up, she says to me, "Good morning, Dan, welcome and how are you?"

Well, she remembers my name, "Great, I am excited to be here". *That kind of weird fever is back again. It's probably just nerves. But this seems different. Can't worry about that now. Have to concentrate.*

"Would you like some coffee, Dan?" Barb hands me a cup and a coffee thermos. "I don't think Earl has gotten to this cup lately."

Earl gets his hands on more coffee than Juan Valdez.

"Cream or sugar?" she offers.

"No thanks, I like my coffee black."

An uneasy first few moments of quiet is broken by Barb, "I like your tie."

"Really? Oh I mean thanks."

"We don't get many ties around here. I mean, none of the staff wear ties. You are going to stick out from the rest of them."

"Is that good or bad?" My head is getting that hot, uneasy feeling again.

And The Name, Again?

Not answering directly, she says, "I want you to meet the planning team; we will be getting together at eight o'clock. After that I will have Ray show you your office. Then you can tell Judy what kind of supplies you will need. Have you met our secretary, Judy?"

"Oh yes, we have met." I venture a humorous note, "She is the one who gives 'coffee clutch' a whole new meaning."

Barb manages a token smile. "Oh here are Ray and Bill now," she says. I recognize Ray, but not Bill.

"Hi, you must be Dave," from Bill.

"Hi Don," from Ray.

"It's *Dan!* Hi Ray, and you must be Bill," I return, shaking their hands.

Something tells me it is going to be a long day.

"We have a lot to discuss; let's get started," Barb begins.

"Dan, we are glad you are here. We have a lot for you to do, but suffice it to say we have a credibility problem. We are at odds with almost everyone in human services at the county, the clients' parents don't understand us, not enough of our clients work in the community, and everyone hates our building. In essence, we need you to develop a marketing program that will turn all that around."

I sit for a minute and then, "Well, I have been told I am a born marketer, so to start with let's consider the building: have you thought of a torch?"

All three roar with laughter. *Thank God.*

"Believe it or not, one of our clients apparently tried to torch this dump a few years ago. But we moved back in," Bill offers.

"We have been looking at space for years," Ray says, "but nothing seems to match our needs."

Barb nods, " I think we are in agreement about our building. Let's move on. Dan, we are going to talk about some things that will make no sense to you, but don't worry, you will get the hang of all of it in time. So just listen and see if any of it makes sense.... Ray, give us an update on rule 38."

Ray starts in about licensing addenda, violations, and waivers, IDT meetings, Human Rights Committee Results, and problems with the county.

Then it is Bill's turn. He talks about "behavioral issues, reinforcers, rule 40 programs...etc."

I have been involved in the computer world and its jargon, in marketing and marketing management, and personnel issues for more than 15 years, but these labels, euphemisms, and psycho babble are new to me. And all this, for people, who according to the staff, have minds of small children.

Again my day dream is interrupted by Barb, "Ray, before all the clients begin arriving, why don't you show Dan his office?"
"Sure, where are we going to put him?"

"Downstairs, in with Bryan."

"But Kris is in there with him. What should we do with her?" he questions.

And The Name, Again?

"Kris doesn't use a desk anyway, just throw her stuff in a box and move her to the front offices down stairs," Bill suggests.

Downstairs. Isn't that where all those people were staring at me? And I get to kick someone out of an office. What a great way to make friends and influence people.

"Let's do it," I nod.

"Dan, I want to meet with you later and give you an official orientation on our rules and so forth. How about 2:00 this afternoon?" Bill asks.

"That sounds good to me," I respond.

"Dan, once you are settled downstairs and give Judy your supply list, track me down and I'll give you a tour and introduce you to everyone," offers Barb.

"Here, let's go down the back steps to your office," Ray directs.

I cannot believe the back steps. They make the front steps look almost inviting. Forget no paint. Check the steps—scuffed, narrow, shaky—a railing would have been a bonus. And then the door, it didn't even have a knob, just a hole big enough for a finger.

 "We could have taken the elevator, I suppose..." Ray muses, "but it gets stuck a lot, or goes straight to the basement and the door won't open. Furthermore, the basement is kind of gross."

It will be two months before I can summon enough courage to use that back stairway again. And as for the basement—four months.

And The Name, Again?

As he leads me down yet another hallway, he unlocks a door and says, "Here is your office."

"Oh..." I survey the a small, crowded room—a desk piled high with papers and books, files overflowing, no windows to relieve the dark paneling. And the carpet...a putrid combination of brown, orange and black.. As I walk around my desk, I trip over something. I look down. A rat trap. Before I ask why it is there, I catch myself—*never mind.*

I haven't even noticed that there is someone else in the room. A guy in his middle 30's.

"This is Bryan," Ray introduces.

"You must be Mister Marketing," Bryan says almost sarcastically.

"Actually I am Dan, but you can call me Mark if you want," I blurt nervously.

I laugh. They stare.

They don't like puns. What if no one here likes my humor? Beginning to panic again. CAN'T make it through the day with out a little levity. Someone is going to have to think I am funny or I'll be more than a little feverish, I'll be dead!

My premature death notice is interrupted by a scream coming over the loud speaker, "George Bush is arriving in the alley in less than one minute." In a flash they are both gone, Bryan yelling, "Nice to meet you, Don," as he leaves to meet the former Commander-in-Chief.

I just stand there staring at my room. Little did I know that

And The Name, Again?

everyone including me will eventually call my office the "Black Hole."

What am I supposed to do now? This is indeed going to be one long day.

I quickly take note of some essential office supplies that I might need for any job and give the list to Judy. Then I look for Barb. I ask her if it is a good time for the tour.

Chapter Three

I'd Rather Have a Root Canal

As we begin the tour through MTS, I really feel like the new kid at school. All eyes are on me. Our first encounter is with someone I had met before. *Now what is her name?*

"Hi Dan, I want to go home."

"Hello Gloria. How are you today?" asks Barb.

Before Gloria responds, I am introduced to clients Ronny, Seth, Zack. Though none speak, they certainly know I am there.

Going toward the dreaded back stairs, I hear wailing sounds and see a familiar face and two very unfamiliar legs. Bill seems to be wrestling two naked legs that are kicking at him. Whoever is connected to those legs is being restrained in a small room off the hallway. The rest of her is pounding against the wall, screaming and crying.

I'd Rather Have a Root Canal

Bill looks at me and shakes his head: "Sam."

I am weak. My fever kicks in again. All I can say is, "What room is Sam in, and how did she get there?"

"They carried her from the alley," answers Barb.

"Does this room have anything to do with George Bush?" I ask her.

"Well I guess it does. When a client is having trouble controlling him or herself, and someone could get hurt, a 'George Bush' is called. Then all available staff come to the aid of the person who is having trouble. If we say that there is a fight on second floor or something like that, all of the clients would come running and we would have a bigger problem on our hands."

My head is spinning. I now sympathize with the first guy who nearly ran me down on the stairway.

I want to run out of this place and never come back. I'll end up institutionalized if I continue working here.

But suddenly a different sound breaks through the confusion in my head. It is a hooting noise and it is directed toward me. I turn to see a small freckle-faced man who from his sounds and his appearance might have been a leprechaun. Though a good 10 inches shorter than I, his startling blue eyes grab my attention and won't let go. For a moment, I feel no one else's presence.

"Tom, this is the new marketing guy," Barb half introduces the two of us.

"What's Tom's last name?" I ask.

"McNamara, Tom McNamara is his name," Barb responds.

"Hello Mac, nice to meet you, my name is Dan."

Mac does not speak to me, but his eyes are putting a hammer lock on mine. I do not know what Mac sees in my eyes; whatever it is he does not want to let go. But he is whisked away by one of the staff, leaving me to wonder if I had passed his "eye exam."

As I am led to another destination, I figure my anxiety level has risen from Panic 101 to Advanced Panic 303. Can I hold on?

The next room is in complete bedlam. Some people are screaming; others are just running aimlessly around adding to the confusion. One person, who seems to be in charge, is trying unsuccessfully to create some kind of order.

"Oh God! What a mess," came from an unidentified voice.

In the midst of chaos, Barb continues her introductions: Mickey, Cleo, Earl, and Arnie.

"Hi Mickey. Hi Cleo. Hi Earl. Hi Arnie. Glad to meet you."

I reach out to shake hands. When I come to Arnie, the in-charge person screams at me, "Don't touch him! He just masturbated all over himself."

My hand jerks back so fast I nearly lose my balance. I swallow hard. Thank God, I didn't vomit.

"Oh that's right, Arnie does that a lot, Dan. I am sorry. I forgot to warn you," Barb apologizes.

I'd Rather Have a Root Canal

I hear no more; my panic level has gone through the roof.

Summoning all the courage I could to speak, I blurt, "I have a dentist appointment; I have to go, be back in an hour."

The next thing I know I am in my car, no coat; it doesn't matter, I am so hot I drive around for a half hour with the windows open in the winter weather. Would they notice if I never come back?

After circling the block heading down Snelling Avenue, I pull over to the side of the road to have a little chat with myself.

Get hold of yourself. What is wrong with you? You are not a quitter. You have to relax and get back to work. It is already almost 2:00. You told Bill you would meet him and besides the work day is done at 4:00. You can hang on till then. "Get back there!"

Walking up the steps, I run into Bill, and he says, "Before we get started, I have to run into my office. Come on along."

As we wind through the second-floor maze, we go through a room that has only one inhabitant. And what an incredibly intimidating inhabitant. He is well over six feet tall, about 270 pounds, and the glare that he fixes on me is not friendly. I manage an extremely weak, "Hi."

He merely stares and grunts.

"This is Randy, he doesn't like people. Don't get close to him. He'll slug you and when he touches you, believe you me, you will feel it. He is unbelievably strong."

I cautiously maneuver around him. *Fine, I will stay away from him. God, what a way to go through life, a self-imposed isolation, with no one around you.*

Bill and I arrive at my office and he starts the orientation. "First, let me tell you about my job. I am the Head Behavioral Analyst. I help our staff put plans together for the participants. These plans entail behavioral, social and vocational goals. Many have behavioral challenges. Many do not speak. Consequently, it is hard for us to know what they are thinking.

Since I have been here at MTS for more than seven years, it has become one of my duties to introduce new personnel to MTS."

His friendly manner and his obvious concern for the clients make him fascinating to talk to. He shares many insights not only into the behavior of the clients but also into the personalities of some of the key people, as well as, into the general politics of the place. It is a lot to think about. I ask him about the clients.

"Can you tell me what they are like, you know, as people?"

He smiles, "They are basically good people who are fun to be around."

But then his smile turns to a most serious look as he continues, "But can you imagine growing up and spending your life—not around people that love you and want to be around you—but only with people who get paid to be with you? No free friends, only ones that are paid for the privilege." His eyes well up a bit.

I am floored. No real friends. I have many friends, people I want to be around and who I believe want to be around me. What kind of a life is one without friends? No, I can't think about it.

Chapter Four

The Pun and the Couch Potato

July

A review of my first few months at MTS: to say they were unpredictable is an understatement; occasionally hilarious is appropriate; challenging and frustrating is accurate.

Oddly enough, the more clients I met, and the more I learned about their lives, the less I understood about autism. Little seems to be known about this clouded, even mysterious, autistic world. Even notable professionals on autism maintain that though many theories exist, many questions remain unanswered.

I believed from the start that I had to learn as much as I could about my clients, if I were to place them in jobs where they could succeed. Few, if any, had vocational success stories. The failure rate was high, and the reasons for their failures seemed as varied as the individuals themselves.

But a major stumbling block could be stated in one word: communication. We needed to be able to talk to a person about appropriate behavior, not only in the workplace, but also in social situations.

Not easy, when the lines of communication are blurred or non-existent.

One such situation arose early in my new career, when I was interviewing a young woman for an intern position. The job would involve assisting me in various marketing projects. In the middle of the interview, I heard my office door open. I looked up to see a client enter. It was Ronny, a nonverbal man in his twenties. I turned to introduce him to the applicant. Instead of shaking her outstretched hand, however, Ronny walked directly to the woman, reached down and with incredible efficiency grabbed the hem of her skirt and pulled it high over her head. I jumped up, grabbed Ronny and literally carried him out of the office.

In spite of my embarrassment, I managed to return to the interview. "I am so sorry; I had no idea he would do that," I apologized. The interview continued without further incident. Though she said she would think about the internship, I think the young woman wrote a "No-thank-you letter" in her car, drove directly to the post office, and mailed it. It landed on my desk the next day.

Later that week, I faced another situation in which Jason, also a client, was to be interviewed for a job opening at Taco Bell. I had been told by his staff person that Jason would be perfect for this position. So I talked briefly to him about it and asked him if he would like to work at Taco Bell. Jason speaks very little, but answered, "Yes." As we walked over to Taco Bell for the interview, he was even quieter than normal. That should have been a signal to me. I am slowly learning in this business not to ignore signs.

The manager of Taco Bell was friendly and polite. She talked about Taco Bell and explained the duties that Jason would have. Then I noticed that Jason was getting a little agitated.

The Pun and the Couch Potato

Trying to soothe Jason's fears, the manager asked, "How would you like working at Taco Bell?"

Jason's face turned bright red. His hands went up over his head. He started clicking his fingers together—loudly by the way—and screamed, "I don't want to work here, I don't even like Taco Bell!" The normally noisy restaurant, though packed with customers, became totally quiet. Everyone was listening to Jason. I was dumbstruck. Two interviews in one week. The first with Ronny, so embarrassing that it seemed to last forever. The second with Jason, though taking about 20 seconds, was equally as embarrassing.

We were about to leave, when another of our clients, who happened to work at the restaurant, came up to me with a desperate look on his face and said, "Dan, you have to help me."

"Sure," I said, "what do you need?"

"You have to take me to see the governor."

"You know him?" I puzzled.

He simply walked away, mumbling something about needing to help the governor clean up the environment. I then remembered that our governor had been on TV the night before, talking about "us doing our part to clean up our state."

On the way back to the office, I looked at Jason. He wasn't embarrassed. He was relieved. With his one-line interview, Jason had made it clear that restaurant management was not one of his long-term goals.

Later, relaying to Bill what had happened, I admitted, "There have been interviews and meetings that I have been stuck in where I knew nothing was going to work out. It would have been fun to raise my hands over my head, click my fingers and say 'Hey, this isn't going to work out—screw it.' Yes, we should all get that chance a time or two in our lives."

There were many other interviews and exchanges, some amusing, some embarrassing, but all—thought-provoking. What are these people thinking? What makes them do things the way they do? The unanswered—perhaps unanswerable—questions nagged at me continually. Then one day something happened that changed my life and our clients' lives forever.

Aaron is one of the first persons I saw at MTS. He stays around the second floor door, watching everyone come and go. He seems to do nothing but stand in the doorway and wave or flap a piece of paper or cloth in front of his face. About 25 years of age, Aaron is a handsome man, who, I was told, is autistic and severely mentally retarded—the mind of a two-year old. Whenever I passed him in the hallway, he would smile and look at me—and flap. At one point, I suggested that we give him a feather duster and let him dust the place. His staff people did not appreciate the idea.

But one day, when he was hanging around with a few other clients in the hallway, I approached them. Although I realized that only a few of them could speak, I asked about their weekend. One volunteered that he had squabbled with his roommate; another responded that he'd gone bowling. Spouting some foolishness, I suggested to them that I had had a very quiet weekend, which led me to make a poor joke. I said that, as usual, I stayed in both Friday and Saturday nights knitting, but then I spent Sunday morning at the "Church of St. Mattress."

Enjoying my own wit, I laughed for those who could not share my pathetic humor. But as I scanned the crowd, my eyes connected

The Pun and the Couch Potato

with Aaron's. He was rolling his eyes and shaking his head. An appropriate reaction for any of my friends, but for Aaron? He understood that silly pun? How? He's not supposed to be smart enough. I have been punning most of my life. Since making people laugh is my hobby, I know when my humor is received, and Aaron understood completely. I was in a state of shock.

Walking down the hall, I ran into one of the speech pathologists, and I told her what had happened. She shook her head. What I had told her made no sense, not with these people. She insisted that verbal humor is very hard for the brain to comprehend. Though I did not talk about it again, the moment was etched in my brain. I could not get over it.

When Friday came along, I was dead tired. Though I usually enjoyed happy hour, I decided this evening to "couch" it, with my TV clicker in hand. Mindless channel surfing was the remedy for my fried brain. Lying on the couch, half in dreamland, I flicked through cable row. Landing on one of those news shows, I heard the word "autism." I stopped.

"What's this?" I wondered.

A woman started talking about the silent world of autism. She explained and demonstrated a new technique that linked autistic people to computers and letterboards that somehow enabled them to communicate. I was no longer prone. I sat up. The more I watched, the more awake I became. By the end of the show, I was standing and shouting at the TV. "This is about us! They understand my wretched jokes! Now they can tell us what they want to do and what they are thinking. We can communicate!"

Chapter Five

Screw You

The next Monday, the first thing I did was track down one of the speech pathologists. I had to tell her about the show I saw and about this technique called Facilitated Communicating, FC for short. A perpetually exuberant person, I was almost bursting when I gave her my glowing account of the news story on TV. But my four-star review got a chilly response from my audience. Why wasn't she as excited as I was? Wasn't I explaining the technique well enough to her?

As I wound down from my euphoric level, she responded, "Interesting. Sure I have heard of FC, but I don't think FC has been proven yet." And she walked away.

I felt deflated. Talk about failure to communicate. I felt as if I were the autistic one and she couldn't understand what I was feeling. Totally bewildered, I walked to my office and sat down. I started to replay in my mind what I had seen on the TV news story. An autistic person had been typing on a computer with the assistance of a staff person identified as a facilitator. The facilitator touched the hand, wrist or arm of the disabled person who pressed letters that came out in words and phrases that made sense. The reporter had also explained that, in general, people with autism did nothing they did not want to do, but they would spend hours communicating with the facilitators.

These people were cooperating as they were communicating. They looked relaxed. They looked as though they were being understood.

"FC," I thought, "hasn't been proven yet? What more proof would anyone need? In fact, what's proven about anything we do?

My reverie was interrupted by the announcement that the staff management meeting was about to start. After the setback with the speech pathologist, I sought some comfort from my associate Bill, who by now had become a friend. I asked him if he had seen the show.

"No. But it sounds like it was really interesting," he said.

"I wish we could find out more about it."

Nothing more was said about FC until the following Friday. I was walking up to our building and Bill stopped me in our parking lot. He was obviously excited about something.

"You aren't going to believe what happened!"

"What is it?" I asked, knowing that when it came to MTS, an exciting event could mean almost anything.

"You know Renee, the new staff person, don't you?"

"Well, I have really only been introduced to her."

"It doesn't matter," he interrupted, "one of her friends told her about FC and Renee tried it with Aaron and Jack. And it worked!"

"You're kidding?"

"No, I'm serious, I was there. Aaron typed 'You have to help me.' And Jack followed with 'Screw you Bill, for not talking to me first.' Isn't that excellent?" Bill was clearly enthusiastic. "Hey, I got to run, but I'll talk to you about it Monday." And he was gone.

I stood there in our parking lot alone. I felt very strange. I was beginning to suspect that fate had brought me to this most unlikely place. My job was not just to help people find work, it was to help them find their way in our world. By enabling them to communicate, their lives would have more meaning, and maybe even a little happiness. All the frustrating times I had experienced at MTS were for a reason. Then, remembering the chilly reception that the speech pathologist had given FC, I realized that I might also be here to fight for our clients.

On the television program about FC, I had seen the expressions on the faces of the persons communicating that could have been exchanged with those of our clients—blank and withdrawn. But on the TV program with the use of FC, those expressionless and distant looks were replaced with a focused and animated presence. They were communicating. And now Bill and Renee had experienced the same thing at MTS.

The fever that had bothered me at Midway was gone. That dizzy, disoriented feeling was replaced by a clear-headed, definitive awareness. I had felt ineffective because I could not reach the people I was trying to help. How could I help them if I didn't know what they wanted or were thinking? With FC, guessing could be replaced with valid choices. Blank stares could be replaced with computerized voices. Wait for the OK of experts? No reason to wait any longer. We've got work to do. Let's get going!

After all, scientists agree that we know very little about the brain. One of the persons with autism had communicated via FC on the TV show: **"Our brain works differently than yours. And just because we do not speak, does not mean we have nothing to say."**

With the ugly MTS building looming over me, I thought, "My God, if my job was interesting before FC, what in the world will the future bring?" But even I had no idea what was in store for the bad punster and his new friends.

Chapter Six

Please, Call Me Mathew

My plan for the following Monday morning was to track down Renee, who like me, was new at MTS. Though her introduction to FC was a few days old, she was still filled with enthusiasm.

"What was it like?" I quizzed.

"It was really neat. My girlfriend had told me about a seminar she had gone to, and she briefly explained the procedure to me. So I tried it with Aaron and Jack. It worked right away with both of them. I took Aaron's hand, held out his index finger. We both looked at the computer keyboard. And his hand started to move first to one letter—then another, and so on, spelling **hhheellppme** (help me). Then I turned to Jack, I asked him what his favorite color was and he typed: **blu**. I then asked what his favorite food was and he typed: **ppiizaaa**.

After that I got Bill, to show him. "I guess you heard about that."

Please, Call Me Mathew

"Would you mind showing me?" I asked.

"Not a bit, how about with Jack?"

I grabbed Bill and we all met in my office. It was quiet there and I had a computer.

I greeted Jack. He gave me a rather cocky-looking glance; he seemed to be saying, "How ya doing?" But Jack does not speak.

Then Renee began with the procedure. She asked him questions about food and color preferences. To each he responded appropriately. He then typed: **i wwannt to ttalk tommom**

Bill said, " Jack, can I ask a question?"

Jack typed: **yy** on the key board.

"How can you read? Where did you learn how?" asked Bill.

"**iiiiu taaauggghttt mmmyselfff**," was Jack's response.

Bill, Renee, and I looked at each other in amazement.

"Can I ask another question, Jack?" said Bill.

"**yyy**," typed Jack.

"Who else can do FC? What other clients can?" asked Bill.

"**alltheeaautistttics**," returned Jack.

Renee, Bill and I were literally jumping around the room. We were

Chapter Six

ecstatic. Meanwhile, Jack sat in the chair patiently waiting to "talk" more.

Unfortunately our discussion was interrupted by an announcement that the van was leaving for the YMCA.

Renee said, "Oh, I have to get going. But I'm going to try FC with some more of my clients. We are going to have to talk about this later."

She hugged Jack. Bill and I both shook his hand. We all went back to our jobs.

At the end of the day, when we met in my office. Renee reported more success with different clients. Bill and I were amazed.

Over the next few days, we met with more clients and a few staff to see if FC would work for them and if the clients were willing to try it.

Amazingly, almost every client Renee worked with, responded very favorably to FC. The few who did not seemed nervous or were "tactilely defensive" (part of their disability was the result of their fear of being touched).

Bill suggested that we had to get more staff involved with the FC technique. He thought that each client's staff person should see what was happening. But most staff were skeptical, some even cynical. It just seemed too easy and how could it be possible? But a few, Christina, Kathy, Bryan, and one in particular, Brad, were really taken with it. Brad was certain that what he saw was real. Period. In fact, he went off on his own, and a few days later, he announced he, too, could facilitate—and with remarkable success. We felt vindicated.

Bill also thought we needed to inform the parents/guardians and also the Board of Directors of MTS. Yes, there was a lot to think about.

I wondered how I could best help the effort. I decided that dealing with the board of directors was my job. Though I was still a newcomer at MTS, I had dealt with the board a few times and received some positive response. I felt I would be quite comfortable pitching the board for approval and perhaps even a grant to expand our use of FC. Furthermore, Bill and Renee would have their hands full, just showing FC to the other staff people. Some of our staff, though very caring, had been trained in behavioral psychology and had come to assume that any skills their clients possessed had to have been taught to them by professionals. They had a lot of difficulty believing that what they were observing was true communication.

Bill compiled whatever information about FC that he could find. He would scan anything that seemed interesting or pertinent and present it to us. From this information, we determined that the research being done by Professor Anne Donnellan at the University of Wisconsin in Madison made the most sense to us and our clients. Donnellan and her team were proposing that many people's problems stemmed from movement disorders. When they want to do something, their bodies might not cooperate to complete the task. Almost from the beginning of FC, they communicated about "getting stuck," meaning that they were blocked from performing seemingly easy tasks.

It was becoming apparent that we at MTS were pioneering many aspects of FC. And somehow that seemed appropriate for us because MTS was founded by the parents of children with disabilities, at a time when there where few such social programs. These progressive parents had been instrumental in the development of many programs to help disabled people.

One of these parents, Leona Deering, is still on our board. When we presented FC to the board for its support for us to continue using the technique, she was an instant supporter. The open-minded attitude of our board and Barb, our president, was vital for us to continue the use of FC. That encouragement further encouraged us to forge ahead—and see where FC would lead us.

Initially, we thought most clients had trouble pressing keys, or touching letters on an alphabet board because of poorly developed muscle and eye coordination.

For example, if we asked, "How are you doing today?" A response might look something like this: **ffffiinneeeee**-for fine. Or if typing a word such as "lunch," they might type it: **lunvh**. Their feel of the keyboard reminded us of our experiences when learning to type. Because they quickly got better and more accurate the more they used the keyboard, cleaning up their text became less necessary.

As for the staff, Renee and Brad were the most proficient facilitators. Personally, I was not successful with FC for about a month. I guess I was too nervous and excited. But I worked patiently with a few clients until it clicked. After that I became good at it and could facilitate with everyone at the center who chose to use it.

The information that people communicated continued to astound us. How could they spell so well? How could people who had so little control of their bodies and who displayed virtually no verbal or even signing skills be so eloquent and intelligent?

Almost daily, Bill, Renee, Brad and I would meet with a client or two in the Black Hole. The more time we spent with clients, the more we got to know them.

Remember Randy, the big one, the self-imposed isolationist? He took quite well to FC. One day he and his staff person Kris were with us. A man who never seemed to want to be close to people was allowing us to hold his hand as he talked to us via the computer.

Does Randy have any physical problems?

he hasgood hearing (Randy had been considered deaf.)

What about your headaches?

they are gone when ontypewriter I get upset when you talk too loud

Randy, can you communicate with other people with autism?

yes with Aaron, Jack Matthew is frightened

We all looked at each other—confused. We knew Aaron and Jack, but who was Mathew? We had no Mathew in our program. So Bill asked, "Who is Mathew?"

dear friends I ammathew I want to talk to you fcr0m inside Ran5dy (Dear friends I am Mathew. I want to talk to you from inside Randy.)

Are you saying that Mathew is the inside person?

yes he is

Does Mathew want to talk?

yers he hurts for long ttime

Is Mathew a good person?

yes h isb he can't control hittoing sorry Renee ad kris
(Yes he is. He can't control hitting. Sorry Renee and Kris)

Which person hits?

randy h9ts mathew is ni ce

Where did the name Mathew come from?

godddd gggave it tome

What is Randy's favorite food?

hur when yo8 callob mje randy
(Hurts when you call me Randy)

(We never called him Randy again—from that moment on he became Mathew.)

What is Mathew's favorite food?

frennch friiies

Mathew's revelations left us numb. We all looked at this big man and saw an even bigger man inside. Not only was he gentle and loving, but he was a human being desperately wanting to be recognized.

The encounter drained us all. To provide a little comic relief I said, "Well, Mathew loves French fries, so do I. I'm buying. Who besides

Mathew and me wants some fries?"

The next day we met with Mathew again. We asked Mathew: Where did you learn how to read?

(Author's note: for the reader's convenience, some spelling errors have been corrected, with punctuation and appropriate capital letters added. But in certain cases, messages are retained in original form. In either case, the words are verbatim. We also use the term FC as a noun and a verb to describe our new form of communication. Even though it is grammatically awkward, it is the term we use conversationally at MTS for a novel phenomenon for which no other accepted vocabulary has emerged.)

I learned when I was young. I learned from school and the world around me. It just looked like I did not understand, but I did. So do the others.

Why does outside Randy hit, and why do you seem unsteady at times?

My vision and personal space get confused. I get startled by certain movements toward me, especially from certain angles. I think I see differently, too. The hits are often a self-defense mechanism.

What do we do that makes it possible for you to communicate?

We are not sure. We think it is the touch. Your bodies are in rhythm, ours our not. You provide a steadying support.

What do you think is the problem?

There is a block. Our brains work a little differently than nor-

mal people's. It is like our inside wants to answer but is blocked from doing so by the inability to get the outside to do what we want it to. I hope that makes sense.

So your hitting is not just a behavioral problem?

No, I do not enjoy hitting others. Not at all.

You say "we," do you communicate with other autistic people?

Sure we do. We communicate on other levels. We understand each other.

Sometimes you seem so serious, do you have a good sense of humor?

Yes I do. The chicken crossed the road to get to the other side.

Chapter Seven

Don't Turn Out The Lights, The Party Has Just Begun

One night after work, Bill, Brad, Renee, and I met in the Black Hole. We talked about how frustrating it was that we were so busy with our jobs that we couldn't spend more time communicating with clients. There was so little time with our busy schedules—it would be nice to get some of the more proficient communicators together. Because they all talked about helping themselves and helping us find cures for their baffling ills, Bill suggested we get them together for a Focus Group. We could work with them together at one time. He suggested that we read aloud from the book *Nobody Nowhere* written by a woman, Donna Williams, who has been diagnosed with autism. We agreed to meet the following afternoon.

The next day we assembled. Among us were clients with histories of erratic, or unapproachable behavior, even violent outbursts. Just getting the group in one room was a challenge, and we were all a little nervous.

Bill explained that he was going to read the following poem from Donna Williams' book:

> *In a room without windows, in the company of shadows,*
> *You know they won't forget you, they'll take you in.*
> *Emotionally shattered, don't ask if it mattered,*
>
> *Don't let it upset you, just start again.*
>
> *In a world under glass, you can watch the world pass,*
> *And nobody can touch you, you think you are safe,*
> *But the wind can blow cold, in the depths of your soul,*
> *Where you think nothing can hurt you till it is too late.*
>
> *Run till you drop, do you know how to stop?*
> *All the people walk right past you, you wave goodbye.*
> *They all merely smiled, for you looked like a child*
> *Never thought that they'd upset you, they saw you cry.*
>
> *So take advice, don't question the experts.*
> *Don't think twice, you just might listen,*
> *Run and hide, to the corners of your mind, alone,*
> *Like a nobody nowhere.*

When he finished, he asked for comments.

(Please note: When we work with our clients in a group, or where there is not a computer available, we use letterboards, sheets of paper with letters, numbers, and the space bar, just as they appear on a keyboard. The letterboard also contains the words "yes," "no," and "stop." Clients point out the letters, and facilitators read the messages aloud and colleagues or the facilitators write them down if they think they should be "on the record.")

Mac was the first to communicate. He is the slightly built man who reminded me of a leprechaun at our first meeting. We placed a letterboard in front of him and I assisted him as he pointed out the letters: **It is so true, it is our world, and it is not reality...**

His talk was interrupted by the actions of another client named Lee. She ran over to the light switch and turned out the lights. The windowless room became pitch black. She was, of course, scolded for doing so and the lights were turned back on. We staff still had a lot to learn.

Mathew responded: **When the lights go out, that is what we see...now there is a window and I see light, I see all of you finally, I see things, I know what they are, but I can't touch them, but with treatment, I am now able to feel.**

Lee then communicated: **When I turned out the lights...the darkness, that is what it feels like. I am very happy to be here** [to participate in the Focus Group]. **It hurt a lot, trying to be better, getting stronger all the time. I have so much to say but there will be time for us to talk more.**

Mac: **Some of the hurt** [that we must deal with] **is that we are intelligent but cannot express ourselves**

Trevor: **The poem is very accurate for our world...Yes I feel** [like running away] **often**. When asked about his outside vs. inside, he responded, **Yes my control of the outside is often hard to control.**

Mac: **Rejection comes from everywhere, it even comes from ourselves. We run as far away as possible. We run to the reaches of our minds.** Asked if it was peaceful there, he answered, **Yes, but it does not exist.**

These are just a few of the responses the poem generated. We now realized that our clients, though they have problems, are intelligent, caring people who are determined to improve their lots in life.

Chapter Eight

Have Letterboard Will Travel

Some of our clients hardly ever went out in the community. Since very few people could understand our nonverbal clients, it seemed to be extremely risky to take them anywhere new. Common concerns and notions of many caregivers were "How would they react?" "Do they seem to like anything new?" "Do they get anything out of it anyway?"

The 8 1/2" x 11" sheet of paper displaying a simulated computer keyboard changed everything. Letterboards are close at hand: in our training rooms, job sites, vans, my car, even my suit coat pocket. If something comes up and a client wants to communicate, he or she can reach or point to a letterboard. The issue is discussed and more often than not, resolved. Furthermore, with letterboards close at hand, it is easy for our nonverbal clients to actively participate in conversations, therapy groups, and other skill-enhancing sessions. We have a number of experiences; the following are but a few that support our motto: **Have Letterboard Will Travel.**

As we progressed with FC, our relationship with Professor Anne Donnellan and her team at the University of Wisconsin grew. She and her team were impressed with what we were accomplishing and suggested we should get together. When we were invited to come to Madison, we accepted. Moreover, we decided that we should include one of our clients on the trip. Though Mathew had a history of being anti-social and violent, he had made great strides since FC. We thought that Professor Donnellan and her team would be interested in seeing him.

We asked him, "Mathew, we have told you about Anne Donnellan. She would like to meet you. Would you like to go to Madison?"

shee caan hhelp ussss yess go

"But can you handle the five-hour trip and will your parents let you go?"

bring board i be ok parents love mathew yess

So during our Christmas Holiday break, Barb, Bill, Renee, Brad, Mathew and I loaded in one of our vans and headed for Madison. Being familiar with Wisconsin and Madison, I volunteered to drive.

"My only request as a driver is that at least one person stay awake to keep me company," I announced to the rest of the passengers. There was little traffic, no snow, lots of conversation and the journey flew by. We were just outside of Madison in a little town called Sauk City when we decided to get something to eat. We pulled into a fast-food restaurant. Apparently a number of people piling out of a van with Minnesota license plates was something of an event in this village which might account for all of the locals watching us as we lined up at the counter. One by one, we placed our orders. Then it was Mathew's turn.

"What will you have, sir," asked the lady behind the counter.

Brad pulled out the letterboard. Using the letterboard, Mathew communicated, **chicken sandwich fries diet coke.**

Being last in line, I was able to observe the fellow diners and the restaurant staff. Most were watching what had just happened and were fascinated. Mathew must have been their first letterboard order. No one spoke a word, but I am quite sure they were thinking: "These people are not from Minnesota, they're from Mars."

We continued our conversations as we ate. The other diners weren't eating; they were watching and listening to us, hanging on every word that was spoken or "letterboarded." Though they seemed intrigued by our communication device, none ventured over to us to ask us about our "space age" board. As we left the parking lot, I am sure that all eyes were on our space ship as we continued our journey.

We arrived in Madison right on time. Meeting Anne in person was a thrill for all of us. She has a reputation of being a pioneer in her profession. One of the crusades that she helped lead was against the use of electric shock and other punishments as forms of behavioral control for people with autism. She worked to convince others that not only were the techniques cruel, they were not effective.

We introduced ourselves to her team and found out that we had encountered some of the same challenges that they too had faced. As Mathew FC'd his background and described his successes since FC, we could feel the emotions rise in the room. As Mathew put it later, **WE TOUCHED THEM.**

Anne told us that very few places like MTS were adopting FC the way we were. She told us more than once that the work we were doing was vital—critical for the rest of the world to see how much progress people with autism can make, if they are understood.

Our scheduled four-hour meeting was going on its sixth hour when we realized we had to get back to St. Paul. But before we left, Anne said that she wanted a photograph of her new friends in front of her Christmas tree. Though everyone smiled and looked happy, no smile could match Mathew's. He truly enjoyed his visit to Madison. In fact, after we stopped for dinner on the way home, all the passengers fell asleep, that is, of course, except Mathew. He kept me awake by making his happy sounds. He remembered my request. To look up and see him smiling at me in the rear view mirror was so satisfying, we coasted home.

• • •

Another of our experiences with the traveling letterboard involved our client Mac, who has had back problems for years. He has been to specialists, physical therapists and now sees a chiropractor.

Mac, as well as his parents, have become good friends of mine. One day when we were talking, his father said to me, "Mac's back problems are really troubling. His doctor says he has no way to get answers to questions he needs to ask. Also, Mac has trouble lying on his stomach and we do not know why. And unfortunately, his new caregiver at his group home, is not really sure that his back problem is real. She thinks he might be just trying to get attention. Do you have any idea what we can do?"

"What if I take the letterboard and go with Mac to one of his sessions?" I suggested. "We have nothing to lose." Mac's parents agreed.

So the next Tuesday on the way home from work, I met Mac, his parents and his new caregiver at the chiropractor's office. When the doctor came in, he said, "I hope you can get some information from Mac."

I showed the doctor the letterboard and briefly explained our procedure to him. The doctor did not seem impressed, but asked Mac, "Why don't you like to lie on your stomach?"

"When I was small, I was left alone in an examination room and someone turned out the lights. I was terrified. Never got over it."

The doctor still seemed unconvinced, but promised not to leave him alone again. Next he asked Mac if he would lie down now. Mac smiled and lay down on the table.

As the doctor worked with Mac's back he asked Mac to tell him where it hurt and what it felt like. When the doctor touched one place in his lower back, Mac's body convulsed and he screamed in obvious agony.

"That's it, that's it, it feels like you are stabbing me with a knife. The pain is overwhelming. Please stop."

The doctor nodded and said that the information helped. Leaving the room, he told us he would be back in a few minutes.

Looking around, I realized that Mac's parents were both on the verge of tears. Also Mac's caregiver was obviously embarrassed for suggesting that Mac had made up the back trouble for attention. As for Mac, he looked a little depressed.

"Mac, you did great, what's wrong?" I asked.

Chapter Eight

"I feel like a baby, I should be able to handle that pain."

"Oh no! Don't be so hard on yourself."

"Mac, did it help to be able to communicate with your doctor?" asked his father.

"Such a relief to be able to tell him about my pain. He has a theory as to what is wrong," he FC'd.

We sat quietly until the doctor returned.

The doctor said, "I have a theory about Mac's back problems." We all laughed. The doctor, though looking a little confused, continued to explain. He described the therapy he had in mind for Mac. He was certain he would now be able to help him.

As we were about to leave, the doctor turned to me and said he was now convinced that our communication was real.

"I have learned," he said, "that Mac has a contented look on his face when he agrees with what is being said about him. He had that look when you read aloud what he had communicated.

Thus, FC has brought our clients much closer to what they term the normal world. Common practices that the rest of society takes for granted, such as traveling to meet new people and learning new things, interacting with peers or conferring with one's doctor, are now becoming available to this very under-served segment of society. I hope that one day letterboards will be as visible as eye charts in doctors' offices.

In the field of Developmental Disabilities the notion that "People just do things for attention" is ingrained in staff. As if trying to be noticed is illogical, bad, or uncommon—we all do it; it's human nature. We must stop judging the actions; and start studying the signals, consequently hearing the message. The clients have a lot to teach us. We have a lot more to learn about the mysterious disorder called autism. Who knows, maybe one day a person with autism will help us travel to Mars.

Chapter Nine

Jack

Through FC, Jack had specifically requested to talk to his mother, so we contacted his parents and explained to them over the phone what was happening and passed on his request. Jack's parents, though extremely active in Jack's life, had quite frankly seen it all—the heavy duty medications, behavioral and psychological theories and programs. They were skeptical. Jack, Renee, Brad and I were waiting in the Black Hole, when Bill brought in some of Jack's family—his mother, father and two sisters. Everyone but Jack's dad, got right up to the computer. There was a lot of aniticpation and commotion. But Jack's father looked as if he would rather be anywhere else than in this room.

I could see out of the corner of my eye that Jack was typing into the computer with Renee's help. Renee was reading the words aloud as they came across the computer screen. She was speaking softly. I could hear, but Jack's dad could not.

Jack typed, **"Mom I want you to know how much I love baking cookies with you at Christmas. I can finally tell you that I love**

you very much. Can I talk to dad?"

Not hearing any of what had transpired, Jack's dad looked at me and said, "I don't even know why I am here. We have been to a million specialists; nothing seems to help." He was interrupted by his wife, "Joe, your son wants you." Tears streaming down her face, she grabbed for her husband's hand.

"Yes, Daddy, Jack is asking for you," sobbed one of the daughters.

I didn't think Joe was going to move. His face turned white. Finally, he summoned the courage to walk over to the computer and to his son.

"**Dad**," Jack typed, " **I love when you call me Cowboy Jack**."

Renee had no way of knowing about Joe's affectionate name for Jack. She looked to the family for verification. All she saw were nodding heads and streams of tears.

Jack continues to make enormous progress since learning to communicate. Though he has more skills than most other clients, Jack has other issues blocking his way. He had been institutionalized for years. When he came to MTS, he was, as might be expected, psychologically damaged. But since Jack cannot speak and uses limited sign language, he had no outlet to express himself in any positive manner.

Now, after a few months working with FC, Jack chooses to attend psychotherapy and finds it very helpful. Because he could communicate, he could get a grasp on his unfortunate past and make progress toward a positive future.

Using the letterboard Jack explained his feelings concerning his

Chapter Nine

new avenue of communication:

> **My life had many self-imposed boundaries. The only people I felt safe with, was my family. Now that I can communicate, I feel safer. I am not afraid to take risks. Though I might not physically be able to protect myself, my will to survive is real strong, much more powerful than anyone who might want to hurt me.**
>
> **Though I do not speak, I have a voice. My friends and my family hear me, love me and protect me. God bless you all.**

As we got to know Jack, we realized that he wanted to be a "regular guy" and like regular guys he wanted a job. Jack explained what being able to work means to him:

> **Working is innate to the human spirit. Being able to contribute to society is as basic as getting up in the morning. Though we may never have our dream job, having a job enables us to dream. What I mean is—sure all people dream, even those who do not work. But their dreams are limited and tilted. Rewards must come to us humans—without them, life has no meaning. Life with no meaning is no life.**

Jack assembles window frames at a factory. I remember the first paycheck that he received. I handed it to him and asked him how he felt. He replied:

> **The work is OK, but the money is mine. I don't have to be nice to someone to get it, I don't have to beg for it, all I have to do is earn it. That is a wonderful feeling.**

From time to time, I give speeches to community organizations, often attempting to convince their members that people with developmental disabilities can be productive contributors to our society. When I asked Jack if he had any words of wisdom for me to share at such a meeting, he offered these insights:

> **Working makes us more whole and much happier. We are not burdens, we are partners. We are not takers, we are givers, we are not needy, we are generous. We are not lost, we are found. We see the future and for us for the first time, it is most bright.**
>
> **If one is pitied, one can not be respected.**
> **If one can work, one can be respected.**
> **If one is respected, one can live.**

A special note: For the above communication, Jack used his own computer—a gift from his parents after the "Cowboy Jack" reunion.

Chapter Ten

Sam

We all had other jobs to do: Bill had been promoted to vice-president, Brad had a big caseload and job coaching responsibilities, Renee also had quite a caseload and I was involved with job sites and other community projects, and was out of the office a lot. Consequently, we only FC'd when we could squeeze it in between other responsibilities.

Even though some of the staff remained skeptical of FC, they remained open minded about it. In fact, we were often brought in to try and help when there seemed to be a critical need for communication. Consequently, the clients began to realize that their efforts to communicate with us were not in vain. If they chose to FC and told us what the problem was, we made every effort to accommodate a need or correct a wrong.

FC was starting to enable real progress, but it was still very new to us. Though FC had worked for Mathew, Sam was considered an even more potentially dangerous client to work with. She had a

Sam

one-to-one staff, who was with her at all times. To be painfully honest, we did little or nothing for Sam. We were just relieved when she did not attempt to hurt someone. It was incredibly ironic that Sam, who always was accompanied by a one-to-one staff person, was perhaps our loneliest client.

The following is Sam's story:

Several months after we began FC with our clients, we were sitting in the Black Hole talking about the day's events when our review was interrupted by Kathy. She was shaking as she said, "Sam went ballistic on the way home. It took two of us with everything we had, to keep her from completely trashing the van, and everyone in it. She was completely out of control. I wish there was some way of getting to her." Then she said, "I'm pooped, I'm going home. See you all tomorrow." And she was gone.

We stared at each other until I blurted out, "Why don't we try to FC with Sam?" They all had that "you have got to be crazy" look on their faces.

I said, "What could she do, kill us?"

"Yes!" they said in unison.

"Oh. But look at what FC did for Mathew."

I was met with total silence.

"Just think about it," I asked.

When I made the suggestion that FC might help Sam, Renee, never afraid of a challenge, volunteered to try it with Sam. Renee and Brad asked her if she would like to try it and she appeared willing.

Chapter Ten

(Sam is not inclined to do anything she does not want to do.)

They sat her down in front of a computer. Renee took her hand.

Renee asked Sam, "Can you spell your name?"

Sam responded by typing the following:

sssaam

Brad and Renee looked at each other in amazement. No matter how often it had happened the first words always give us a huge thrill. Brad said to Renee, "Ask her to spell your name."

Renee took Sam's hand and asked her, "Sam, can you spell my name?"

Sam typed: **bbbiittcchhhh**

End of session one with Sam.

Renee and Brad reported the story to Bill and me at the end of the day. Needless to say our reactions were mixed: amazement, humor, and concern. Sam, too, had been misunderstood. There was someone intelligent behind her beautiful blue eyes. She was not empty-headed. This woman could respond to communication. Obviously, she also had an attitude—and not a positive one. We all wondered, could we help her, did she even want help?

A few days later, I worked up enough nerve to try FCing with Sam, I asked her staff person if I could take her to my office to see if she would facilitate with me. Though he looked at me in disbelief, he agreed to let me take Sam.

Sam

I asked, "Sam can you spell my name?" Keeping in mind her response to Renee, I should have thought better of my first question.

yy dabbnn

I was calming down. Sam seemed to relax. She looked as if she wanted to type some more. Sam will speak a few words—very occasionally. So I asked, "Sam, do you have something else you want to say?"

She said, "Yes."

I took her hand, she went right to the keyboard.

"yoouu arree gooddii aaamm bbbadd"

Instinctively, I asked, "Do you want to be good, do you want to change?"

y

"I will help, what can I do?" I followed.

listen

With that response, she got up and walked to the door. I wasn't sure I had enough energy to walk with her. A woman, who had terrified and maimed many who are more capable than I, was asking me for help. But my assignment seemed possible. I could listen.

Over the next few months, Sam and I met regularly. The more she FC'd, the more verbal she became. For example, through FC and speech she indicated that she had horrible dreams and was often extremely disoriented. She also explained that she had a temper (no kidding). If she were petrified, confused, or angry, she would act out. But Sam was changing. Sam was more relaxed, often pleasant and comfortable. The number of her outbursts decreased. Everyone (staff, clients, the people where she lived) noticed. Sam was mellowing. The only variable that changed in her life was that people were listening to her. She was being understood.

Like all of us, Sam has had setbacks, but everyone who knows her, sees a dramatic change over the last couple of years. She loves to work at our center—regularly receiving a paycheck. She goes on outings in the community much more often and interacts with other clients in Social Skills sessions.

Let Sam explain it in her words via, the letterboard:

> **Dan I want you to know that it was your help and faith in me and God that enabled me to pull myself out of my horrible world. Thank you for that and thank you for sticking with me. You were the only one brave enough, and you never gave up on me. God bless you for that.**
>
> **I feel good. Not feeling bad all the time has changed my life. I dream of the future no longer in nightmares, but of hope and excitement. My life has meaning now. My friends mean everything to me. I can now love them, because I love myself. God is wonderful. He didn't give up on me, I got another chance. What a wonderful break we all get. I have no intention of wasting my second chance.**

Chapter Eleven

Arnie

You may remember Arnie. He was the straw that almost broke me, on my first day at MTS.

Yes, Arnie could FC. He was a warm, thoughtful fellow who had friends at MTS, and though he had trouble controlling some of his actions, his warmth shone through. In fact, the more interaction we shared, the more comfortable he became in the company of others. He cared and gave us encouragement to continue the FC project.

As Arnie became more proficient with FC, he had fewer behavioral problems. While he talked about life in a most reflective way, he gave us no indication that his end was near. Arnie died of liver cancer in November of 1993. But he left us in style.

After Arnie's malignancy was diagnosed, he became weaker and weaker. He could only sit in his wheel chair. In fact, as we watched the staff load Arnie onto a bus one day, we all thought it would be the last time we would see him alive. We didn't see him again until one day, about noon, the elevator door opened on the third floor.

Out rolled Arnie. He looked weak and tired, but we were very glad to see him. Actually, we were surprised that he was able to make the effort to come.

Suddenly Brad remembered the date. Arnie's birthday! We moved fast and held an impromptu birthday bash in the Black Hole. We were there, Arnie's buddies were there, and of course, Arnie. No cake, but I quickly whipped up a batch of Arnie's favorite: popcorn. Everyone rallied to show Arnie how much we thought of him, but he could sense our sadness. When Arnie had seen enough of our sad eyes, he motioned to be wheeled over to the computer and he communicated the following:

> **You are some of finest people I have ever known. Do not be sad. The only sad thing would be if I couldn't have spent my final birthday with the people I cherish most. I am going to be your special friend in heaven. Let the party begin.**

It was his birthday, but we received the gift.

Arnie died a week later.

Renee, Brad, Bill and I attended Arnie's funeral. Arnie's home of over 30 years was not what the normal person would call a home—it was an institution. Many of its residents, who were as the system puts it, "extremely behaviorally challenged," literally had grown up in institutions and state hospitals. When we arrived at the church, we were pleased to see that every other resident from Arnie's place was there. Funerals can be tough and I openly wondered how everyone was going to handle Arnie's service. When the service began, the congregation was silent. But as the music started, the only distracting noise we could hear in the church, was coming from the so-called normal people, who were sobbing, as the rest of his friends sang good-bye to Arnie.

Chapter Twelve

FC Half-time Update

December

December always seems like a good time for reflection. It gives us a chance to sit back, review the preceding year, take stock and make plans for the future. As I watched the snow fall outside the window of my new office, I was reminded of the many good and not so good things that happened to us the past year. Two examples of the good: the windowless black hole is no more and we moved into our new facility in March.

The beginning of the year was an exciting time for us. Our clients' improvements were becoming apparent to many—to our staff, case managers and parents. In fact, MTS was beginning to be recognized as a progressive, innovative place where great advances were being made by some of the county's most behaviorally-challenged individuals. MTS was on the right track.

Half-time Stats

People Working:
- 98% of eligible clients working
- 60% of eligible clients working in the community (including an unheard of 50% of people who are considered behaviorally-challenged)

Our clients work in a variety of capacities in the community. Some are housekeepers in hotels, assemblers in a factory, restaurant workers, clerical workers, and bed makers in nursing homes. These jobs may not seem glamorous, but they give workers a sense of self-respect and purpose. Oh yes, they can also buy things. All in all, a pretty normal reaction to a paycheck?

A county representative described our ability to place the behaviorally-challenged in community-based work as "unprecedented, outstanding, and commendable."

Staff Who FC'd: The list has grown from 3 to 10, almost one-fourth of the staff.

Clients Who FC'd: Though almost all of our clients showed the ability to FC, some chose not to use it. About 30 clients, almost one-third, regularly FC.

Behavioral Problems: The number of clients' outbursts that required interventions decreased by more than one-half.

Sam, for example, who had a history of being placed in a "Time Out" room up to 3 times per day, went for months of less than one

FC Half-time Update

separation a week! Even before our holiday break in December, she was only isolated in "Time Out" 2 to 3 times a week. December has always been a difficult time of the year for Sam and for many of our other participants because of the holidays and the loneliness of being separated from family.

We define "time-out" as when an individual is isolated in a room to prevent the person from hurting others. Serious aggression on the part of the client must be occurring to warrant the separation. A person may only be isolated from others for up to one-half hour at a time. If a client is attempting to hurt him or her self, staff people must step in and prevent it by holding the person. Time outs may only be used as a last resort. We feel they are dehumanizing, but necessary when violence is occurring and can be curtailed by no other way.

There are so many stories and updates. I can't mention them all, but I must tell you about Gloria and Earl. Remember them? Gloria was the one who greeted me at the door and told me she wanted to go home. Well, she is doing fine, she is living at home with her mother. She recently started a new job in the community and does well. She also is involved with our choir. Though she does not always sing out loud, when we look at her face, we know that she is singing with her heart—on the inside.

Earl, the coffee "clutcher" has flourished, too. Since he suffers a bad reaction to coffee, his doctor doesn't want him to have any.

I asked him one day why coffee, the state fair and clowns were so important to him.

Coffee makes my empty heart feel warm.
I love the rides at the state fair.
When I twirl around in a circle I feel normal.

> Clowns get to go on the rides whenever they want.
> Would you twirl me around when I say clown and point to myself?

So I do. About once every couple of weeks he will run up to me, point at himself and say, "Clown." I gently twirl him a couple of times, he looks at me, signs "Thanks," and walks away.

With communication, Earl tells of his empty heart and his loneliness. I think being able to talk about this has helped. Earl has really made strides, he uses other forms of communicaton including a book of symbols and he signs. He is more involved in the community. Earl loves going to the YMCA to exercise and works well in the community at his job and now only occasionally will he slip and steal a sip. But more importantly, staff have come to realize that Earl's stealing of coffee is not a simple case of "bad behavior" but quite possibly, an uncontrollable urge, or a rebellion from oppressive and unfair restrictions that have been placed on him. Nor does he have to be restricted to the once-a-year visit to the state fair; instead he can readily feel like the energized, ever-popular clown—the prince of our Midway.

Yes, we moved into a new, more inviting facility, and no, the rat trap stationed by my desk did not make the move. In theory, people with autism do not do well with change. So a move, though viewed by many as positive, was not necessarily so for some. But most of us quickly settled in the new facility. Being understood was having an extremely positive effect. People labeled as profoundly autistic and retarded were benefiting from their ability to communicate. Some of us unofficially adopted the philosophy of "Presumed Competency," because through FC we learned that they understood us, our directions, our advice, our efforts. They knew what we were talking about. As one of our staff put it when she realized this, "Oh my God, they heard and understood everything we ever said in front

FC Half-time Update

of them. Gosh, am I embarrassed."

Please note: Her reaction is consistent with other staff—including her tears. We urged all staff to join our conversations, but the wheels of change move slowly and we felt we could only push so hard. Eventually, we hoped, they all would come to our new way of thinking.

County case managers and parents began to request visits to MTS. More importantly, they liked what they saw. Prospective clients were lining up to see our program. For the first time in MTS history, we reached our capacity and started a waiting list.

The new facility raises everyone's morale and has space to provide all kinds of activities, interventions and accommodations to support people. But the key difference was the growing sense of connection between clients and staff that communication was generating. We felt that MTS was on the right track.

But elsewhere, problems began to surface. Court cases involving FC were dragged through the media tabloids. Most laboratory testing of FC's validity failed. The negative press, lawsuits and inconclusive testing had a devastating effect. Nationally, some professionals who supported FC retreated behind disclaimers, and some caregivers were scared off by the possibility of lawsuits.

But the most damaging effect by far was a television documentary that presumed to expose FC as a hoax. Worse, it was presented by PBS in its prestigious *Frontline* Series, which most viewers regard as particularly trustworthy. A group of us gathered at Brad's home to watch it. To say that *Frontline's* conclusion concerning FC was negative was an understatement. The program implied that people who believed in it were well-meaning but were unwittingly guiding people's hands to the letters. In other words, even worse than a hoax, FC was dangerous, giving rise to unfounded accusations of abuse by guardians and care staff, and taking people away form worthwhile educational and vocational programs.

We sat there in shock and disbelief. The researchers completely dismissed FC because it failed a "double-blind" test. (An experiment in which the facilitator and the communicator view two different pictures. The communicator is asked to type what he/she has seen. The response typed most often was the picture viewed by the facilitator not the communicator, thus indicating facilitator influence.)

The "double-blind" test only confirmed what we already knew. To a person, even our highly verbal participants, have trouble remembering concrete facts, and especially when they are being tested. We were not using FC for that. We encourage the use of picture boards and signing for that kind of communication. But no form of communication was better than FC for letting us know how they were feeling; what was bothering them; or how we could help them. FC enabled us to really get to know them. Accommodations they recommended and insights they shared with us via FC were having positive results, to say the least. As far as we were concerned, the dramatic improvements in the quality of life they were enjoying, carried more validity than any laboratory test.

Furthermore, the show's experts insinuated that any improvement in behavior or progress of clients were for other reasons and that believers of FC were basically unrealistic, undereducated and were "desperate for a cure." MTS had followed the most popular behavioral-management models recommended by experts. The conventional wisdom maintained that with volatile clients, following behavioral models to the letter was critical in keeping "control." To be honest, we sensed that behavioral models were keeping staff and clients at arms length and *fostered* control issues. How could anything be fair when only one side makes the rules and the other has to live by them, whether agreed to or not? It was becoming very clear that an environment based on control had to be replaced with one of cooperation, and communication if our center was to become a community.

Furthermore, our former disciples of behavior modification, Bill and Brad, readily admitted that dramatic improvements by clients were rarely accomplished with their programs. But now, with open channels of communication between clients and staff, profound improvements had become commonplace.

As for facilitator influence, of course we knew it exists! In what form of communication is there no influence? But we *used* our influence to create an environment where clients could feel "free" to communicate without fear of indifference or recrimination. Though vulnerable, they are not helpless. In fact, they had been remarkably helpful in assisting us to support them in improving their quality of life.

Moreover, unfounded sexual allegations were used to heighten the drama of the show and to negate the validity of FC. The fact that some persons, who have been accused, tried, and convicted of abuse were identified by FC was never discussed. Nor did *Frontline* mention that nonverbal people are more vulnerable to abuse because ordinarily they cannot complain or confront their victimizers. With FC there was a chance that imbalance would be righted to some extent, but in fact, there had been relatively few allegations given the number of new communicators. Of the tens of thousands of people using FC, only a handful of people have ever accused others of abuse.

The *Frontline* show ignored the many examples of information brought out during communication that the facilitator could not know about. The issue was not even brought up, much less discussed. The entire show was biased and unfair.

On the way home questions raced through my mind.
*Could I be completely wrong? Not about FC. I know it works.
Was I imagining things? No! Look at all the positive results.
Was I scared? Yes! But of what?*

I drove for a while longer, looking at the stars. Then it hit me, I realized what really scared me.

I have grown to know and love these people and they me. If I could no longer communicate with them, I am afraid I will have to leave them. If I turned off their right to communicate, I could never face them again. Return to a place where these people are considered helpless and incapable of telling us what or how they are feeling? No, I simply cannot go back to that!

The turbulence was felt throughout MTS. Though enormous progress had been apparent to all, several of our staff persons backed off, and others began to question FC. It was a blow but was it a death blow? Was the MTS FC train derailed?

Once again we looked to the parents of our clients for direction. We asked them, "Do you want us to continue with FC?"

Only one parent asked us to hold off for a while. Another, who seemed to speak for the majority, put it this way, "Our son is happier than he has ever been. If we parents had to wait for every professional and researcher to give something new his or her seal of approval we would never have made it with our children. No, you must continue with FC!" MTS remained on track.

So while there has been some open skepticism and outright rejection of the notion that FC is a valid means of communicating, MTS is not in the business of proving anything. Rather, we are seeking to improve peoples' lives, enabling them to achieve their potentials. It was obvious from the start that FC was having a dramatic effect. Behavior problems have plummeted. Many people who rarely left the center are now working in the community.

Do we believe that FC is real? Of course we do. People prove it to us every day. Through FC they have told us things about themselves that we would have had no way of knowing. We check later and find out that the information is accurate.

For example, when one of our clients seemed listless, we were wondering what was wrong. We asked him and he FC'd to us: **I can't sleep when it is completely dark. I need a night light on**. Bill called his group home and asked a staff person about a night light. When she said that there was a night light in the hallway, Bill asked her to check the bulb. Sure enough, the light had burned out. She changed the light bulb, and the problem with fatigue was solved.

In another instance, when one of our clients was not eating, I asked him what was wrong. He communicated through a letterboard that he was having pain and thought he might have an ulcer. We informed the group home; a staff person took him to the doctor, and yes, he had an ulcer.

Then there was also the time that Ronny came to us very upset. When asked what was wrong, he communicated that he had "gotten into it" with one of his staff people at home. Our staff person called Ronny's home to get more details about the confrontation. Her question concerning Ronny was met with, "How did you know about Ronny's fight? Who told you?"

But that kind of proof is only part of it. They are growing, no longer merely existing. The reason is simple. They communicate. Mathew was asked, "Are you happy?"

On the letterboard he communicated, **"Before FC we existed, just existed. But now we can join your world. It makes us more whole."**

Since they could now be understood where they had been previously so misunderstood, we agreed that their remarkable stories had to be told. Many of them have been labeled with a mental age of two and an IQ below room temperature. But our clients—who more and more are our friends—though they have problems, are far from immature. In fact, the term incredibly thoughtful is probably more appropriate.

Chapter Thirteen

Leona is Endearing

"Raising three normal children and four disabled ones was the last thing I thought God had in mind for Leona Deering. But apparently God knew I was a war horse who never backed down from a fight. Particularly a fight when I thought someone was being taken advantage of."

I first met Leona at one of our board meetings. A striking woman with snow white hair, she herself is disabled with severe arthritis. She walks with a cane; on bad days, she uses her wheel chair. Though she looks younger than retirement age, a simple math test considering the ages of her children in our program would establish a golden age for Leona. But, you would never guess it. She gives piano lessons, substitute teaches, and sits on several committees for people with disabilities. And a few of those committees she either organized or helped to establish. She rarely misses one of our board meetings, and is always at least 15 minutes early, wanting to know this or that about the program. And not just about her four children in our program, but about all of our participants. I knew that she had been associated with MTS since it was founded in the 1960's. I think it is safe to say, "She has seen it all." Yes, she is vocal, not afraid to challenge and to make sure that the motive for change is for the betterment of the clients.

One of the perks of working at MTS is that I get to meet and befriend some wonderful people. I think you might enjoy learning a little about the members of Leona's family who attend MTS.

The day after I interviewed Leona, I ran into her oldest daughter Maggie. Maggie communicates verbally. I told her that her mother and I had had a great talk the night before. To which she responded, "Hawkeye, our cat, liked you didn't he?"

"Well, yes, he did. In fact your mother told me that Hawkeye doesn't warm up to many people."

"I knew he would like you. I love Hawkeye."

Later that day, I ran into Alice, Leona's youngest daughter, and I told her how much I had enjoyed my time with her mother. She nodded in understanding and appreciation.

"I met Hawkeye too," I offered.

Alice, who speaks very little, looked right into my eyes, and with clear enunciation said, "RAT."

Ally and I roared with laughter.

Leona's oldest son is Carl. He is a gentle man, whose life revolves around music. It can either energize or relax him depending on his needs. I asked Leona about the role of music in her family.

"When our children were growing up, we had music playing constantly. I mean 24 hours a day. Not radios blaring or loud, wild music. But music that had a good beat and rhythm helped the kids get motivated, get relaxed and, believe it or not, even get to sleep. Nothing could help change the mood or regain order faster than music. It is Carl's godsend, and I guess it has been mine, too."

And Joe, her youngest. While Carl is the quiet music lover, Joe is the gregarious people lover. Though he speaks very little, he loves to act and to entertain.

"Oh, yes. All my kids were raised surrounded by people. Our disabled kids had the same expectations and privileges as our others. They were always included in functions and the rules were simple. Act respectfully and politely, and you will be welcomed anywhere."

Think about it—two sisters, two brothers, so alike, so different—so normal.

When I interviewed her for this book, I knew the answer for the question that I was about to ask, but I wanted to hear it from her.

"Why do you worry so much about how the clients may be affected by almost any decision?" I asked.

"Because the only reason MTS exists, is to make the lives of the people we serve more meaningful. Period!" she fired back.

Chapter Fourteen

"I Love To Pound On Dem Keys"

One of the most interesting arenas for FC has been in Group Therapy. Our psychologist has worked with people with developmental disabilities for years. At the time we started using FC at MTS, Dr. Antonello, or Dr. Steve, as he is affectionately known by us, lost his father unexpectedly. He held one of his Social Skills therapy groups but said nothing about his loss. To his surprise, one of the clients came up to him and said, "Your heart looks heavy and your eyes look sad."

On the day of his father's funeral, he stopped by to see one of his clients. He was in no shape to hold a therapy session so he talked for a few moments and decided to reschedule the appointment. Before he left, however, another client offered an audio cassette for him to listen to. To his amazement, when he played it in his car on the way home, he found the music was cued to his father's favorite song.

At the funeral, Steve relayed these stories to Bill and me. Bill and I looked at each other and smiled.

"I Love To Pound On Dem Keys"

"We too have some interesting stories for you," I said. "When you come back to MTS next week, let's talk."

The next week, Steve came to see us after a Social Skills session. Steve told us how touched he was by our clients' kindness and "awareness."

Bill and I had planned our talk with Steve. We wanted to impress him with some of our encounters with FC, but we did not want scare him off. We caught his attention with a couple of interesting revelations made through FC. He listened, taking it all in, but this man has the proverbial poker face. I couldn't tell if he believed us or was ready to refer us to one of his respected colleagues.

"Interesting," he admitted. "I have to run to an appointment, I'll see you Thursday. I would like to know more about it."

After Steve left, Bill and I looked at each other and smiled. He had taken the bait. Maybe, just maybe, he would let us incorporate FC into his work with clients.

A few weeks later, Dr. Steve returned to MTS for a Social Skills session. He stuck his head in my door, and he said, "Let's try that FC stuff today. Can you join us?"

"Yes, I'll get a letterboard and meet you in the group therapy room."

As I walked into the room, all those assembled had their eyes on me as if they had been waiting for me. Dr. Steve told the group that we were going to attempt FC with anyone who wished to try it. Steve went on to say that the day's topic was going to be "What do you do when you are sad?"

"I Love To Pound On Dem Keys"

The group consists of 12 of clients who vary in communication abilities. Some talk and some use sign language. As he was working his way around the room, getting responses to the topic, he came to a woman, nicknamed Jess. She is a woman in her sixties, visually impaired, a very pleasant person. When she was asked the question, she answered, "I never get sad."

Although I knew very little about Jess, I ventured, "Oh, come on, Jess, you must get sad every once in a while."

She did not respond. Instead she reached across the table and placed the letterboard in front of herself. Lifting up her index finger, she turned to me. It seemed to me, she was saying, "Let me talk, let me be heard."

I walked over to her, touched her index finger, and she started pointing to letters on the board. She typed the following: **"when I am sad, I love to pound on dem keys."**

After I read it aloud to the group, I looked at Steve. He asked, "Jessica, what do you mean?"

She very softly verbalized, "Piano."

Steve said, "Jess, there is an organ in this room, would you like to play for us?"

She said nothing, but went over to the organ, turned it on, and started playing *Rock of Ages*.

The group erupted. Jess smiled; she had a completely different look. Poised, confident, serene.

I was amazed, I had no idea she had any musical talent, much less

"I Love To Pound On Dem Keys"

the ability to play so beautifully. Neither did anyone else in her audience. No one wanted her impromptu concert to end, so I asked her if she did requests. She nodded yes.

"Do you know one of my favorite songs, *Roll Out The Barrel?*" I asked.

The true crowd pleaser she is, she played it perfectly.

After her third encore, Dr. Steve thought it was time to move on. We had yet to hear from some of the others.

Rich, a man in his sixties, who seldom speaks, was next. He reached for the board. Lifted his finger. I took his hand. He typed the following: **Wwh3en I amm saad I thinmk of my frttiends**... Then he stopped, put his hand down and started talking, "who have died. I play their favorite song on my stereo, and sing it to myself. And then I am no longer sad."

I was startled. Never before, had anyone typed out words, stopped mid-sentence, and started to speak. I looked at Steve. Consummate professional that he is, Steve usually gives an appropriate response. None given—only a tear in the corner of his eye.

Several others also chose to use the letterboard. It became apparent that these clients, although somewhat verbal, felt more comfortable confiding more private thoughts on the letterboard. The entire atmosphere and emotional climate of the session was heightened, yet comfortable. The discussions were serious and moving; the responses and encouragement from peers were encouraging and compassionate. People chose to take risks and used FC to open up. Their disclosures were met with understanding and open arms. As I walked Steve to his car, he said it was the best session he had ever had at MTS. He couldn't wait to try FC with our other groups.

"I Love To Pound On Dem Keys"

A few months of using FC in the Social Skills Sessions really opened our eyes to the participants. As they became more communicative by using the letterboards, they seemed more determined to be to improve their lots in life through therapy.

One example of how dramatic our sessions became can be illustrated by Abby's story. Abby is a woman in her early thirties, speaks little, but knows the words to every Beatles' song ever published. I guess we knew she related to music, but we had no idea to what extent.

One day in group, Dr. Steve was going around the table asking people about how they felt about friendship. When Steve got to Abby, she gave no verbal response, but pointed to the letterboard. I put it in front of her and she typed: **Haacvve him sibng me the qwuedstion.**

I repeated her response to the group.

Steve immediately sang to her, "Abby, how do you feel about friendship?"

Usually Abby has to be asked a question 3-4 times before she responds; but after Steve's solo, she sang back, without hesitation, "I love my friends, many are in this room."

"Would you like to ask them a question?" sang Steve.

Abby turned to another client in the group and sang "Shane, I hope you are my friend."

"Abby, yes you are my friend," Shane harmonized.

"I Love To Pound On Dem Keys"

Steve and I just looked at each other. Their duet may not have been Lennon and McCartney, but it was certainly music to our ears.

If I ran into Abby in the hallway and I said, "Hi," to her, only rarely would she respond. Now, when one of us sings a question to her, she will appropriately respond in song almost every time.

At the end of that dramatic session when we discovered that Abby could easily sing her responses, Dr. Steve sang to her, "Abby, what is your favorite song?"

"I am woman hear me roar, too big to ignore.......," Abby sang. Helen Reddy would have loved it!

Chapter Fifteen

Welcome Back, Son

Remember Aaron? He's the one who understood my joke about St. Mattress. His major activity had been standing in the hallway or in his room flapping paper in front of his face. He communicated that he flaps to calm himself down but he can get "stuck" doing it and he can't stop. He asked us to help him flap less. So we encourage him to flap for only a short period of time, when he feels he is becoming agitated.

Now that we understand each other, his life has changed. He told us that he could work and that he wanted to work. With the assistance of our speech therapists and occupational therapists, we developed a realistic plan that he understood and agreed to. With the support our staff is able to provide, he works in an assembly plant. He also does our laundry. He says he loves the feel of cloth in his fingers. He is saving some of the money he earns for a trip to Florida. He says he dreams of swimming with dolphins. For recreation he goes to the YMCA, and regularly goes out to lunch with his friends.

I'll never forget the phone calls with Aaron's mother. I had not met his parents; all I had been told was that they weren't too involved in his life. But they were still his guardians and I needed their permission for some extra on-the-job training we wanted to provide for Aaron. So I called them and reached his mother. I started out the conversation by introducing myself and informed her that I worked with her son. I went on to tell her what I needed and she agreed. But then I told her how much I enjoyed Aaron, and how much fun he was to be around. She seemed bewildered. She asked me, "How do you know all this?"

"I FC with Aaron, and we have become good friends."

"Oh, okay," she returned. And she hung up.

A few days later, the phone rang in my office. I picked it up; it was Aaron's mother. She wanted to come to see us.

"Tomorrow?" she requested.

Knowing she had not seen Aaron in years, I hesitated, "I guess so."

When she hung up I went to tell Aaron. He was not pleased.

"What's wrong?" I asked.

"I wanted to be better at FCing than I am. I wanted to be where you just touch my shoulder and I can type," he communicated.

Aaron had been progressing very well with FC. Staff people touching him at the elbow could enable him to communicate on the letterboard or computer. Apparently, he wanted to be even more convincing. But after Brad and I talked with him, he relaxed and looked forward to seeing his parents again.

Welcome Back, Son

Aaron's folks arrived the next day—an hour early. Aaron was still at work, so I stayed with them for awhile. They wanted to know more about FC. I told them that I use it with Aaron. When they asked for more information, I told them that Renee, Bill and Brad would be great resources and that they would be in shortly.

Both parents seemed very nervous.

"They took Aaron from us when he was four," Aaron's mother blurted. "I never thought he was mentally retarded. Different but not retarded. No one would listen to me."

"We just did what the doctors told us we had to do. Aaron gets very upset when we come and see him. It's not that we don't love him, it just hurts to see him get so upset," Aaron's dad followed.

Sensing their pain, I hoped the visit would make them feel better. "Nobody knew," I thought to myself.

We just sat quietly until the rest joined us.

I had to leave for another meeting, but when I returned after an hour, Aaron's mother was talking. "For the first time in so long, we have good news about Aaron," she said. "Look how great he is. You people are wonderful."

Aaron's dad waited for her to finish. His eyes full of tears, he added, "You have made us very happy. We have our son back."

The next day in Social Skills, Dr. Steve asked Aaron how he was doing. He typed, **"A perfect ten. Yesterday was the happiest day of my life. I have my family back."**

Chapter Sixteen

Padre Knows People

I had met Padre Johnson, the illustrator of this book, through a mutual friend. Padre, artist, author and world traveler, was having an exhibit of his Global Family paintings in St. Paul. When we were introduced, he asked me what I did for a living. I told him that I worked with people diagnosed as autistic. As I gave him a five minute review of my experiences, I became aware that he was demonstrating a more than ordinary interest in what I was telling him.

"I have been in almost every country in the world and there are people with autism everywhere. I know little about them and would love to know more," he said. "Would you be willing to bring some of your clients to my exhibit?"

"That'd be great. I'd love to," I answered.

We set a date for a private showing in order that Padre could spend a some time with our clients. He wanted to get to know them.

Two weeks later we headed for the exhibit with four clients and five staff persons aboard the van. I was sure that they would have no behavioral problems, but because of the value of these paintings, we included the five staff people. We were going to take no chances. Furthermore, each client who came FC'd, so I wanted to make certain that we had enough "hands" to assist our clients. I knew Padre would want to ask them some questions, and I was also quite sure we would have some.

As we walked into the exhibit, Padre came right over to us. He immediately turned to Mathew. As they were being introduced to each other, an instant bond seem to form. Mathew and the rest, if you recall, don't usually take well to strangers. But this was different. Mathew began his happy sounds, and rubbed his hands together. Padre reached out to shake both of his hands. They just stood there for a few seconds, smiling at each other.

Everyone walked around, studying the portraits. The clients were clearly fascinated. After a while, we sat down and Padre began to tell us of his travels around the world and the wonderful people he had met. Then he welcomed questions.

Mathew, FCing with one of our staff, asked, **"How does it feel when you draw?"**

"The life of whom I am drawing, comes right through my fingers."

Aaron was the next to ask, **"What do you see when you see the sky and water?"** I was assisting Aaron and honestly did not know what Aaron was talking about, but Padre knew.

"My friends, the blue of the sky and the water is seen in every face I draw, we are all born to this planet. We are all a part of this earth" said Padre. Aaron nodded that he understood. I responded, "Oh."

The questions continued. And they continued to impress Padre. He and our clients seemed to be on a plane different from the rest of us.

Padre Knows People

Knowing little about art, I was trying to pick up as much as I could from the discussions going on around me.

Padre started talking about the Bushmen of southern Africa, the people on whom the movie *The Gods Must Be Crazy* is based. He said, "The people are the most wonderful I ever met. They love, nurture and respect each other like no other society on earth. They don't even have words in their language for hate or murder."

He continued, "You people have that same peacefulness and sense of goodness that is far too rare in our world today." As he choked back tears, he continued, "Please forgive me for being so emotional but I feel a love and appreciation for life in this room that I seldom feel. This visit has meant a great deal to me. Thank you for coming."

As the last of Padre's visitors were loading into the van, he grabbed my arm. "These people touched me, may I come and visit them at your center?" he asked.

I knew he was serious. "Sure, but with your busy schedule, when would you have time?"

"I'll make time. Here is my phone number; please call me tonight to set up a visit."

We drove back to our center in a blinding snow storm. Normally when I drive, all eyes are copiloting our journey, but not today. The clients all slept. As we made our way along the slippery highway, the staff exchanged their reactions to the exhibit experience.

"Everyone was so into Padre's art and his stories. They asked such deep questions. I'm blown away," said Ray.

"They would look at the paintings and then look at the descriptions that went with the paintings. They were getting it. They knew," from Kathy.

"They listened to every word he said. You could tell they agreed, too," Renee chimed in.

"Padre is really impressive and he saw something in us. We could have stayed there all day," said Helen.

Chapter Seventeen

Reject the Expected

One thing the new communicators told us from the beginning of FC was that they wanted us to be firm but fair with their "outsides." That is, they wanted us to understand that though some of their actions were beyond their control, they still needed addressing. There was a huge range of such behavior: Mac became "stuck" in doorways, Ronny had an unusual fixation with snapshots, and Ray had conversations that were basically limited to repeating the words of others. Each person's difficulty was essentially unique.

We all became so conditioned to such actions or inaction that they were almost viewed as typical behavior for the clients. In essence their behaviors were expected and more-or-less accepted. Through the use of FC, we learned that these were not just bizarre and quirky behaviors, but were some time accommodations that they developed in order to maintain a degree of calmness or to avoid periods of agitation. They were trying to help themselves.

Furthermore, they acted certain ways, not to misbehave but because they could not avoid the behavior. Being stuck is different from being stubborn. With FC, clients told us that they wanted us to help them overcome these actions.

Mac, for example, suffers from extreme disorientation when walking from room to room. He can become paralyzed, stuck, unwilling or afraid to move. We used to think he was just being stubborn. No, he is locked. To repeat, being stuck is much different from being stubborn.

We received the most help with Mac's problem from the experts—the clients themselves. At an FC Focus Group we brought up the problem of being stuck. We asked them for ideas that could help. They suggested that imagery, more commonly known as visualization, might release him and others from such difficulties. Imagery, defined by our clients, is the ability to look at oneself in a successful or inspiring endeavor. It can break the feeling of being stuck, unsure or afraid to proceed.

Of all of us, Bill seemed to know the most about imagery. He had heard of it being used in a variety of ways, but he knew we needed to do more research. The more we looked into it, the more obvious it became that imagery was used by many different types of people, but everyone seemed to use it for roughly the same reasons. Athletes, for example use imagery for "raising to the next level" and overcoming obstacles. Diet and other self-help programs use imagery for people to see themselves in a better light and to overcome adversity. We were coming to the realization that perhaps the very brains that seemed to be at the root of their problems could in fact be, the brains that could help them with some of their baffling issues.

Mac wanted to address his problem of not being able to pass through doors from room to room. He gets stuck and freezes either one side of the doorway or once he has made it into the next room, he has to return to where he was, and not where he would like to be. We call it "transitioning from place to place."

We sat down with Mac, I took his hand as he reached for the letterboard. He started pointing to letters and explained his image to us, it took him about ten minutes to type out what he was visualizing. He imagined himself a Minnesota Twins baseball player. It is the bottom of the ninth, score tied and the Twins are down to their last out. He is up, and cracks a homer. As he is circling second, headed for third, he waves to the screaming crowd and is greeted at home by his teammates. They all congratulate him. He and they win the game.

Mac hoped imagery would break the "feeling of confusion and disorientation." He explained that his natural space is distorted. He becomes afraid that any movement will make him lose his balance. But the daydream-like feeling that is his image, allows him to become "unstuck" and enables him to focus. His image seems to bring him from a sensation of vertigo to orientation and sure-footedness. When Mac becomes stuck, we remind him of his "game winning" image and that usually enables him to proceed through the doorway. Mac gets stuck less often. But when he does he can use a second strategy that he developed for himself—a quick spin sometimes lets him cross the threshold. If that doesn't work we remind him of his baseball successes.

Another client, Ronny, when he becomes agitated (which is often), calms down by looking at photographs. But once he starts looking, he has trouble stopping. Looking at them becomes an addiction or fixation. The more he looks, the more he wants to look. He also communicated a desire to overcome his problem.

To help Ronny wean himself from the habit: We gave him a stack of 15 snapshots when he appeared agitated, and told him that after he looked at them he was done. He seemed relieved, and it worked. Gradually he looked at fewer and fewer snapshots and those less frequently. He became much better-natured and more comfortable around others. This new confidence aided him in overcoming another of his problems.

Ronny, if you recall, was the skirt raiser—the person who, when introduced to a young woman I was interviewing, ignored her attempted handshake and proceeded to raise her skirt over her head. On the letterboard, he said he acted that way to keep people from getting too close to him. Close touching by others made him feel as if he were being smothered. He knew if he took the offensive, people would avoid him. His actions helped by keeping them away, but also hurt because he was alone. Now he feels more at ease with others, can tolerate a hand shake and is no longer lonely. I don't think he has used the skirt greeting in over a year.

A further note: Ronny is an artist. One day, I noticed that he had sketched a striking picture of a tree in autumn. I asked him, "Is autumn your favorite season?"

He nodded.

"Why?"

He typed, **"ALL GODDDSS COLLLORSS"**

When I told him that I hoped he was going to give the picture to me he looked troubled. "What's wrong?" I asked.

Ronny typed, **"PPARENNTS CHRISTMSS"**

We framed his autumn scene and wrapped it. I made sure that it was under their tree for Christmas morning. I'm sure that the picture was not their only gift, but I would guess none was more precious.

Ronny now works at our center, but he has dreams of being a

photographer and an artist. He no longer wants to look at pictures, he wants to create them or paint them.

With accommodations being so successful, we started looking at many "behaviors" in a different light. Perhaps, we thought, other troubling conditions could be improved or rectified. Glen is a prime example of looking at an age-old problem, with a new attitude, and seeing a promising new future.

Glen echoes the words of others. Initially, conversations would proceed in this manner:

> I would say, "Hi, Glen. How are you?"
> Glen would respond, "Hi, Glen. How are you? Glen's fine."

He could not explain why he repeated, but he did not like doing it. It was as though he felt the words of others were more acceptable than his own responses. But it became a crutch for him, an accommodation on which he became too dependent. I think that he thought echoed conversation was better than no conversation at all.

We worked together to overcome his problem, to build his confidence in his ability to converse with others. If Glen repeated my question or observation, I would say, "No. I don't understand that response." Gradually, we progressed from a "How are you today, Glen's fine" response to "I am fine."

When a fellow staff member watched me work with Glen, he seemed puzzled.

"I thought he had to mimic. I didn't think he could just answer," Tom said. "I'll work with him too."

It is a slow process—but Glen has had success with direct

conversation. With his new-found ability to converse with others, Glen works in the community. Also, he has revealed an interest in music and art, which our staff is helping him to develop.

• • •

The following comment made by a client named Ted is significant and in more than one way: "If staff expected us to get stuck in a certain behavior, we would usually get stuck." Perhaps that statement may also be true when the expectations of staff and clients are reversed. To illustrate: At Ted's annual meeting, the staff of the group home where he lived was talking about the previous year and making plans for the following one. The discussion was about weekend activities, what to continue and what to change. Ted had been getting pizza every Friday night. The staff thought that since he seemed indifferent to the pizza, perhaps another Friday night activity was indicated.

Ted reached for a letterboard and demanded to be heard. **"DON'T TAKE MY PIZZA AWAY, I LOVE PIZZA."**

The surprised staff responded, "Since you never seemed to enjoy it, we thought you didn't care for pizza."

"IF YOU KNEW I LOVED IT, YOU WOULD HAVE MADE ME EARN IT."

End result: Ted got to keep his Friday night pizza—but more importantly, he helped his caregivers become "unstuck." By showing them how inventive he actually is, he brought to life how "stuck" they were with unfair and unimaginative programming. Their negative practices had no positive effect on the person they served. And though we don't know what long-range impact this episode had on the residential staff, once more MTS staff were reinforced that the clients are the key stakeholders and that they must be included in all phases of the program development process.

Chapter Eighteen

Cruise (Not Bruise) Control

Many disadvantaged individuals are controlled and trapped by rules, regulations and procedures initially developed to help them. In fact, "being controlled" often hurts people by denying them basic choices and freedoms and socially retarding them.

Labels like developmentally disabled, mentally retarded and vulnerable adult, tend to create attitudes that cause people to be treated as less than human. Many behavioral management techniques employed, are oriented more toward regulation and control than to communication and support.

The MTS approach has always been to strive toward positive relationships but there is no doubt we became handicapped by the hierarchic model that places staff in control of clients. Nevertheless, as the months went by, more of our clients communicated their feelings and their dreams to us, the less we had to deal with Presidential visits—remember the call for "George Bush?" The number of crisis interventions dropped dramatically. But when the call does goes out, the heart still skips a few beats in anxious anticipation of what awaits us.

One morning about 10:00 a.m. I was working at my desk, when over the loudspeaker, I heard "George Bush! We have a George

Cruise (Not Bruise) Control

Bush in the garage. Dan Reed, please go the garage immediately."

I grabbed a letterboard, and as I raced to the garage, other "George Bushes" flashed through my head. To have one of our clients upset and out of control is not only painful to see, but is also heart breaking to feel. I want to cry for everyone involved. We always hope to restore order without injury or loss of dignity. Not knowing what was going on or who was having trouble, I just hoped I could help.

As I entered the garage, I saw Sam being held by four or five staff people. She was screaming, spitting, hitting and trying to bite. Bill was attempting to hold her hands, but she was still able to lunge at him and hit at everyone she could reach, including herself.

"We don't know what is wrong. Would you ask her what the problem is?" asked Bill.

Sam seemed to be on the verge of going completely berserk. To counter her hysteria, I knew I had to appear calm and confident. In order to find a way out of this situation with resolve and dignity, she had to have faith in me.

"Can I take your hand, Sam?" I asked, slowly reaching out to take her hand. Instinctively she tried to grab me, but Bill spoke quietly, "Sam, Dan wants to help; you don't want to hurt him, do you?"

"No," Sam said ever so faintly.

Though she was still kicking and trying to rip Bill's clothes, I took her hand. She seemed to calm a bit.

"Sam, what's wrong?" I asked, placing the letterboard in front of her. She immediately typed, **"New staff, introduce me, I worth it. Yes."**

Cruise (Not Bruise) Control

I repeated what she had typed. "Did she get a new staff or something?" I asked.

"Yes, I'm the new staff. She's right; no one introduced us to each other," responded Kelly, nursing a bruise on her head. "Is it any wonder she wanted to get away from me? She didn't know me from Adam and she's supposed to trust me? I don't blame *her*."

It clicked with everyone at once. "Nobody introduced Kelly to you, Sam? We're sorry. Sam, this is your new staff person, Kelly. She will be working with you." said Bill.

Sam calmed down further. She FC'd, "**Hi, sorry**." And then a few moments later she said softly, "Fine."

She may have been fine, but we were exhausted. The experiment worked: meltdown averted, no one seriously hurt or further embarrassed, and Sam was properly introduced to her new support staff.

Kelly, came up to me a few days later and said, "What you did with Sam was unreal. It turned her right around. Honestly, I was skeptical of FC until I saw for myself how well it works. Thank you."

"I still get the chills when I think about it," I said. "It was pretty amazing wasn't it? Just being able to communicate stopped her downward spiral."

"Sam was fine with me the rest of the day. I think she and I will get along."

Despite our complete lack of sensitivity, Sam made the effort to tell us what was wrong. She rose above our shortcomings and defused a potentially explosive situation. I wish I could say we consistently do the same for her.

The information we were learning through FC has been invaluable. Sam's actions were for a reason, not because she felt like acting like a baby, but because she felt she was being treated like one. Whether her actions were caused by an involuntary loss of control or her display of rage was intentional in order to achieve her goal is a moot point.

Perhaps if we included Sam in more of the decisions that concerned her, she would have been more in control of herself. In the future people like Sam will help choose staff to work with them.

With FC it is much easier. Such procedure may sound elementary. Being mandated to support and protect a vulnerable person is a major responsibility. It is not a license to do that person's thinking or to take total control of that person's life. Unfortunately, many people with disabilities are governed by rules and regulations that are well meant but result in controls that diminish their stature as human beings.

Any time someone in power decides what another person needs—that is control. In Sam's case, the social amenities (the courtesy of a personal introduction), which *we* have come to expect as a matter of course were overlooked. The result: Sam fought to be recognized—at least she had the strength to assert herself and enough faith in us to hope she might be acknowledged.

Unfortunately, people who cannot communicate conventionally are more likely to be ignored and either break and give in, or resist and fight. When they give in and allow themselves to be ignored, I believe they also become less inclined to think, more inclined to withdraw; less likely to flourish, more likely to stagnate. Ironically, when persons such as Sam act bad to be noticed, the system often comes down harder on them and further restricts their lives. When others in society fight to be heard and to gain their rights, they are hailed as being determined, brave, and courageous freedom fighters. When unheard people with disabilities seek the same respect and dignity, they are apt to be labeled uncooperative, non-compliant and behaviorally challenged.

Chapter Nineteen

You Can See Better If You Get Close

While this book is mainly about our clients, the work of our staff cannot be ignored. To give a clearer picture of some of these efforts, I will reintroduce three persons to you: Dr. Steve, the psychologist in the "Love To Pound On Dem Keys" chapter, Kathy, the staff person who survived the wild van ride with Sam, and Bill, then the Head Behavioral Analyst, who gave me my MTS orientation on my first day. These three are examples of staff who have become close to our clients.

MTS serves more people than just those who have been diagnosed as autistic. Some other diagnoses are Down syndrome, mental retardation, mentally ill with mental retardation, Tourette syndrome (diagnosed and undiagnosed), seizure disorders, and cerebral palsy. Most of our non-autistic clients can speak. We have found, however, that it is to everyone's advantage to promote interaction between everyone, regardless of communication ability.

Social Skills sessions with Dr. Steve are prime examples of such integrated meetings. Though Dr. Steve could usually get a conversation going with some of the clients, nothing had as profound an effect on them as when people using FC began disclosing their inner feelings. Our verbal clients became much more comfortable revealing their feelings.

Nick, a social skills regular explained it this way, "They (the non-verbal people) said what we were afraid to say. None of us are retards—we count. We now talk because you finally hear us."

Author's note: Before we started to "finally hear," Nick rarely had anything positive to say or considered having a job and making friends as possible. Nick has since graduated from group, manages much of his own finances and now car pools to work with a co-worker, and on nice days they come to work by motorcycle. He even volunteered to give a speech at the Holiday party.

When I went up to thank him for his touching speech at the party, he said "Thanks, ya, I did O.K. But, Dan, hey I got to run, the guys from the plant are here and we're going to have a beer. See ya!"

Getting to see Nick and the others succeed is incredibly rewarding. The closer we got to Nick's issues, the less dramatic they became. And now Nick is getting to where he wants to be, and we get to watch him from the sidelines, cheering him on.

Listening to clients was proving just what some staff people and parents suspected all along. Though these people have disabilities, they have many capabilities that have gone unnoticed or acknowledged. Though some staff had been missing the messages, others had assumed capabilities all along, and Kathy is one of the best example of the latter.

Kathy headed up our in-house contract work and believed that everyone is capable and should have the right to be stimulated, and to work if he or she chooses.

She told me the following shortly after I started at MTS, "It is much more effective to build a rapport with people; it makes it much easier to work with them." She went on to say that enabling our clients to feel good about themselves was critical before they could feel good about their lives and the lives of others.

But hearing the messages we were hearing via our new communication surprised even the most forward-thinking. She, like many others, took what we were learning and modified her behavior toward clients even more. The great results motivated *us* to further accommodate and to jointly set expectations. That is, we were coming to a level playing field where we all expected performance—individually and as a team.

One day an incident happened that illustrated Kathy's rapport with her clients. One of Kathy's clients asked Kathy and me if she could tell us how she felt about one key topic: respect. Chrissy, a 30 year-old adult with medical problems, mental illness, and classified as mentally retarded is, nevertheless, a proficient typist. Now she is receiving computer training at our center. Recently, she typed the following:

This is about Respect and getting along with others.

If you want to be treated with respect, you have to give them respect. If you want to be treated like an adult, you have to act like one. If you don't give them space, they won't give you space. If you are rude to others, they will be rude to you...
You have to respect their rights, or they won't respect your rights. I would really like to see people respect others around here at work. I want to see respect, responsibility and adult-like behavior and to have friends.

Kathy extended herself to build a rapport with Chrissy, encouraging her to speak with confidence about a subject important to her.

We continue to build on the way that Kathy instills expectations in all of us. People, who may have seemed indifferent to most activities, are beginning to take the first small steps toward more productive lives, and now many of her clients have jobs for the first time in their lives. And perhaps more significantly, staff, who saw no point in building a rapport with people they serve, are seeing Kathy's attempts pay off, and are beginning to following suit.

Bill has a philosophy similar to Kathy's. He began his career in the early 1970's at age 16. He started working with the "hardest of the hard" at a large state hospital in southern Minnesota. This experience had a profound effect on him: the staff were indifferent at best, the environmental conditions appalling, and the mistreatment of residents commonplace. However, Bill saw in the eyes of society's rejects the seeds of hope and a glimmer of love.

After college, he went back to work with the people whose survival amidst adversity had impressed him so much. Now "properly" schooled in the technology of Applied Behavioral Analysis, he could write and implement programs to decrease severe behaviors and increase adaptive behaviors. But according to him, something was missing this time around. Where was the humanity? Where was any sort of meaningful life experience? Even though he felt he was making a positive impact on the lives of a few people who lived there, he continued to be disillusioned with the cumbersome and demeaning state system.

He came to MTS in early 1986 looking for a place where innovation was encouraged, risk-taking rewarded, and the positive elements people with disabilities possess recognized. But nagging questions continued to bother him:

- What if everyone you were exposed to wanted to change your behavior?
- What if your very existence centered around other people's idea of right and wrong, good and bad, valuable and useless?
- What if the extent of your choice making was limited to the most mundane of life's experiences?
- What if the only people in your life were there because they were paid caregivers?

Bill's goal was to put humanity back into Human Services. Even though the principles of Behavior Modification were valuable, his success with the most difficult of clients was, in his mind, directly attributed more to his caring touch and ability to work with people than any well conceived program plan. Bill talks of exposing his own vulnerabilities by speaking with people and connecting with them at a personal level. When Sam bangs her head so hard on the wall that holes result, he hurts. When Sam successfully applies a label to an envelope, he rejoices. He terms this "parallel emotions." I think it is being human. When we employ empathy and love, progress in life becomes a cooperative venture in which both parties benefit.

Synthesizing information that we obtained through FC, we collaborated to develop motivating and challenging goals and objectives. As a result, more people are working, there are fewer occasions when people lose control of their behavior, and more positive interaction of clients with staff. The MTS community still has challenges and problems, of course, but we are dealing with our clients on a different plane. With our client input, Dr. Steve's insight, Kathy's ability to motivate, Bill's work in behavioral programs, as well as the work of the other staff, we are enjoying progress. While our successes can easily be overstated, the quality of life at MTS has been greatly enhanced.

Chapter Twenty

The Christmas Gift

It is not often that people at MTS get a chance to go out and enjoy themselves.

We sponsor dances and parties at MTS and have our monthly All Company meetings, but rarely do we get to socialize together outside of work. At our annual holiday parties, we get the opportunity to interact with each other on a purely social level. We do it right—rent a hotel ballroom with a sit-down dinner, gifts and dancing.

Furthermore, we receive recognition for our accomplishments during the year with such awards as: Most Improved, Most Positive, Best Attendance, Worker of the year. . . But this award ceremony is like few others that I have attended. Never have I seen such genuine enthusiasm. As names are called off, people who are given little credit for reacting appropriately bound up to receive their awards. Proud, honored, and just plain happy to be recognized for a job well done. Something else happens here that should be noticed: when winners' names are called off, the others clap, scream approval and are sincerely happy for them. There is a sense of togetherness, respect, and appreciation for each other—the winners and the "yet-to-be recognized" winners.

The Christmas Gift

It is important to mention here, that the holidays are typically our clients' LEAST favorite time of the year. The reason is obvious. Few have much family contact—most do not have the happy family or childhood memories that we usually associate with the Christmas season.

One of my duties as Marketing Director is to make certain that events, such as the holiday party, go off smoothly. It is one of my favorite duties. I greet everyone and I make sure everyone has a picture taken. It is their party and my gift to them is to help make all feel appreciated.

My second-year Holiday Party was especially memorable to me. To begin with, I was amazed that everyone seemed to be there, even Mac, who has trouble with sounds, came and stayed. This despite the fact that, as he had indicated to me, the noise was "driving him nuts."

But when the dinner was over and the program began, everyone, including Mac, seemed comfortable yet unusually excited. The awards ceremony commenced—Best Attitude, Most Creative, Hardest Worker, etc.. . . I was busy taking the winners' pictures when they came to the category—Staff Employee of the Year.

As I was getting set to take the winner's picture, Kathy nudged me and said that she wanted to see the camera. I said, "Now?"

"Yes, now."

"The employee of the year is Dan Reed," announced Barb.

I was flabbergasted. For a fleeting second, I felt like that Oscar-winning actress who said something like, "You like me, you really

The Christmas Gift

do."

I looked around. Everyone was enjoying my reaction to my unexpected news. Frankly, I knew the clients liked working with me, but the staff? It is an interesting mix of personalities and backgrounds, but the common thread in everyone is that we all care about the clients. As you might imagine, I have had disagreements with some of the staff, but they must have recognized that as far as I was concerned—the clients must always come first.

I have never been accused of being a man of a few words—until that night. All I said was, "Thank you all very much. I am very lucky. But I have a question for you. How many people do you know, who can say they have gained a hundred and twenty great new friendships in the last two years? Well, I can. Thank you again, my friends."

As the party was winding down, I saw that Mac and his family were preparing to leave. I went over to the table to wish them all a Merry Christmas. Mac caught me with his eyes. He obviously had something he wanted me to know.

I said to him, "Thanks for sticking it out. I know the noise really bothers you. I hope you had a great time."

I pulled out my pocket-sized letterboard for him to respond.

" nnone of us woould hve misssed this for anything. This is your parrtty tthaank youiu."

After I hugged him and his parents good-bye, I stood there alone for a few moments and realized, "What a wonderful gift, this MTS."

Chapter Twenty-one

"Ouija Board" or Letterboard?

Is Facilitated Communication real, or is it some sort of unconscious process of the person assisting the client? Are we, the facilitators, merely guiding hands to letters? Although, they have told literally hundreds of things that we would have had no way of knowing and indeed the information is verified, critics still have trouble acknowledging that FC is authored by people labeled retarded.

Through FC, we have learned a lot about our new friends who have been diagnosed as autistic. They have shared with us their likes, dislikes, dreams and fears, beliefs and concerns. From that information we have "dialogs" that have enabled us to get to know each other. We have gone far beyond the usual client-staff relationship, to much more of an equal, normal partnership. No longer viewed as needy, helpless, disabled people, but seen as caring, human, aspiring people who want a better life for themselves and for others. Though they still have vulnerabilities that mandate us to protect them, they are, we have found, readily capable of helping themselves and others, if given the chance.

FC has also enabled us to better understand their independent attempts at communicating. Nonverbal communication such as

"Ouija Board" or Letterboard?

signals, signs and gestures had previously gone misunderstood, unnoticed or ignored.

Jack, for example, has a way of showing us when a topic in a Social Skills session is too difficult for him to discuss. He puts his head down and "appears" to be too tired to participate. He explained that if a subject is painful for him, he needs to listen to the others first, and then he may be able to reflect on the topic and resolve a few concerns. He said to us, **"Don't throw me out."** He was paying attention.

Mathew, whose given name is Randy, told us, " **Randy used to hit a lot.**" But it wasn't because he was mean. He was easily startled. If someone surprised him, he might strike. He told us that his slapping was a warning to stay away or back-off until he could gather himself. Before FC we didn't know when he became agitated, whether he was going to go on some rampage and hit people, or hurt himself. And, of course, our response would be to get in his space, to protect him and/or others. Mathew communicated, **"Just give me room to breathe."** Now we do. Almost with out fail, he calms down in a few seconds—no interventions, no head-butts, no more loss of dignity. The once widely-feared Randy is now the much-loved Mathew.

One more example from Mathew. At work one day, he stopped doing what he was doing and fussed a little. In the past days, he would have been hauled away, probably never to see that job again. Now we can ask him what was wrong.
"The lights are bothering me. Move me please," he FC'd.

We moved him to the other end of the table out of the glare of the florescent light and he went right back to work.

Aaron, who has shown the most "visible" progress, uses many

ways to communicate nonverbally. Aaron has two jobs now. One is at our center and the other is in the community, both are important to him and he takes them very seriously.

Aaron is fiercely independent; he has worked on communication gestures to the point that he can nod appropriately to yes or no questions. At his job in the community, Aaron prefers not to use the letterboard. He wants us to ask him yes and no questions. When asked why, he typed, **"ber likke otherss"**

He wishes he could talk, but being understood and respected means everything to him.

Since FC, Aaron's behavior problems have disappeared when he is with us. However, his behavior at his group home, though much improved, was not as acceptable as the home staff wanted. One of his residential staff people put it to me this way, "He (Aaron) just acts naughty to get attention."

From the description of Aaron's actions at home, it seemed likely to me that he was rebelling from the strict behavioral regime that "governed" *his* house and that he was no longer going to accept being treated like a prisoner.

We suggested that they FC with Aaron and find out what the problems are. But his residential staff questioned "that FC stuff," and contracted a visit by a consultant to observe Aaron at MTS. The consultant arrived at MTS unannounced. He demanded to "observe Aaron and this FC thing." Since Aaron happened to be working at MTS that day, the consultant was taken to see him. When introduced to Aaron, the consultant did not look at him. Instead he addressed our staff person, "I want to see him do some of that FC stuff. Let me see, where are my notes? Oh, yes, what did Aaron do last night?"

"Ouija Board" or Letterboard?

Aaron typed, **"I WAS BORED,"** with the assistance of a facilitator.

Since little goes on at the house where Aaron lives, his response sounded like a reasonable assessment of the evening's events. But not to the satisfaction of the consultant.

"He obviously doesn't even know what he did last night. My notes say that he watched TV. That is all I needed to see," he announced, as he packed up his things to leave.

"But, you never gave him a chance to get to know you, or you him," said an MTS's staff, "Can't you take a minute and listen to him?"

"Yes, let Aaron tell you about himself. What's the hurry?" chimed in another staff person.

"What's the point?" shrugged the consultant.

He turned away and left without looking at his patient. If he had, he would have seen a very proud young man standing in front of him—crying.

The consultant was accepting only one answer. Had he pursued the matter with just one more question, he might have learned that Aaron indeed had found a TV show "boring."

Clients who have been labeled "severely and profoundly retarded and autistic," as children are often doomed to wear this pathetic badge throughout adulthood. The diagnostic tests that require speech and dexterity to complete may be inadequate, even discriminatory, when given to nonverbal, motor impaired persons. It is true that FC may not be a perfect form of communication, but the results we have seen since it has been introduced to MTS cannot be ignored or dismissed. That would be unfair and irresponsible.

Ironically, some people who have dedicated their lives to the less fortunate have become part of a complex, confusing system based on control and constriction, rather than on accommodation and support. As one of our client's parents said, after observing some of the results of FC: "I don't care if FC is Voodoo, you have to keep doing it with my child. She is so much happier and more self-confident. She is like a different person. Come to think of it, if FC is Voodoo, I think the world could use a little more Voodoo."

Bottom line: FC helps people. "Ouija board" or letterboard? It's your choice.

Chapter Twenty-two

Since We Have Your Attention

The more we worked together, the closer we became. Roles and labels became less defined and less important. True partnerships replaced staff-client relationships. Mathew and I, for example, worked at our relationship like all friends do. Though we agreed on many things, we definitely had differences of opinion. We made a pledge that we did not always have to agree with one other, but we always had to respect each other's opinion. Communication is a right not a privilege, and we would never shut each other out, regardless of how much we might differ.

That basis of mutual respect has spawned terrific friendships. When we had time to sit down with each other, we were like any other friends and co-workers. In many ways, our conversations resembled any group of friends sitting around a table after eating, enjoying each other's company. Bantering back and forth.

By now it should not surprise you that our discussions are spirited, enlightening and sometimes disturbing and moving. The following examples of information shared in our discussion groups reveal insights that these once considered "outsiders" possess.

We start with Alice's comments that were recorded on the

computer and are reproduced. The other clients used letterboards and their remarks are transcribed from the facilitator. Comments and questions of the facilitator are set off by //.

Alice

Alice: **DAN I WANT TO TALK ABOUT SEXISM IN SOCIETY**

/Define, please/

SEXISM IS THE DOMINANCE OR CONTROL OF THE FEMALE GENDER THROUGH MANY WAYS AND TACTICS AND NO IT DID NOT ALWAYS EXIST. IN SOME SOCIETYS THE SEXES ARE EQUAL PARTNERS

SEXISM IS A FEAR THAT THE CHILD BEARER THE ONES THAT BRING LIFE INTO THIS WORLD WOULD NEVER PUT UP WITH STUPID WARS AND SUFFERING THAT WE PUT UPON PEOPLE. MOTHERS WOULD NOT ALLOW THE INSANE SLAUGHTER OF PEOPLE IN THE WORD OF HONOR

BY ALIENATING ONE HALF OF THE PEOPLE OF THE PLANET AS REALLY BEING SUBSERVIENT YOU ACCOMPLISH MANY THINGS. YOU PERPETUATE THE BULL SHIT THAT MEN ARE SUPPOSED TO BE STRONGER. GIVE ME A BREAK. BLIND STRENGTH IS NOT ONLY WORTHLESS IT IS DANGEROUS AND PARDON THE PUN A MISCARRIAGE OF JUSTICE TO THE HOLDER. THERE IS NO REASON THAT MEN SHOUD BE MENTALLY STRONGER TO HANDLE WAR AND OPPRESSION. SEXISM ERODES THEIR SELF-CONFIDENCE AND

FORECES THEM TO BECOME PAPRT OF A CROWD THAT GATHERS STRENGTHF FROM OTHERS. IT ROBS THE MALE OF EMOTIONS THAT MEN DESERVE TO UTILIZE IT ACTUALLY WEAKENS THEM.

THIS IS KEY TOO BECAUSE ONCE ONE LOSES ONE OR MORE OF HIS EMOTIONS FEELINGS INTUITIONS ETC THE WHOLE MACHINE IS OUT OF SYNC.

/Solution?/

THINGS ARE GETTING BETTER EVER SO SLOWLY. THE PROBLEM WITH MANY WOMEN IS THEY TRY TO COPY MEN IN THE WORKPLACE. GREAT THAT IS JUST WHAT WE NEED, MORE SHALLOW SHORT RANGE MORONS. NO NOT GOOD. ONLY WHEN WOMEN AND MEN ARE TRANSPARENT IN OTHER WORDS WHEN GENDER IS INVISIBLE IN THE WORKPLACE WILL WE START USING OUR COMPLETE DECISION MAKING SYSTEM TO TACKLE PROBLEMS AND FINALLY START TO BE NOTICED AND TO BE HEARD.

SEXISM IS A SYMPTOM OF SOCIETYS OPPRESSION OVER OTHERS. YOU KNOW THE HAVES AND THE HAVE NOTS THE BATTLE OF THE SEXES IS REALLY A SMOKE SCREAN OR AN AMUSING GAME FOR THE HAVES TO PLAY ON THE HAVE NOTS.

Mathew

Spirituality

/Define, please/

Spirituality is a life that parallels ours. It is our higher self, working along side of us. Spirituality is a presence or feeling or a set of beliefs that make the human being whole. Without spirituality, the human starts to deteriorate very quickly. Yes, Dan, you are seeing the parallels to autism. Autism is a signal to the human race that without true spirituality we will wither and shut down. We will escape to a reality where we think everything is safe and good. In reality, the opposite is true, and it is a false world full of make-believe happiness and an emptiness that rots the very core of us and our world.

Spirituality is like anything else we learn to use; the more you utilize it, the less you need to use it. Your soul becomes so much a part of you that access and direction are instantaneous.

Mac

Faith

Faith is a word that is magic because without faith very little is possible; with faith anything is possible. Faith is the bridge between your heart and your brain and ties it back to the higher power. Like a computer system, it is your operating system. It is really needed to do much of anything and with a powerful system, you can accomplish some pretty amazing tasks.

Faith, too can be lost. Look at us, the autistics. We lost our faith and were incapable of fighting off our struggles to survive in the "real" world. We have paid the price ever since. Remember when Mathew said we chose to run? We did. The autism decision is an inside decision.

Just a few more thoughts about faith:

Blind faith is bologna. God gave each of us a brain. We must use them. Even sheep are expected to make choices. Furthermore, blind faith is an excuse not to think.

Faith is a power that is contagious; that is why leaders rise from among us. People want to believe and will mimic people with faith in causes, ideology, etc. That is why the abuse of faith is many times tragic and very sad. It leaves the victim vulnerable.

Faith will save humanity and without it we have nothing. That is why when people lose faith in governments, they fall. Unless we believe that our faith will get us out of the hole we have dug for ourselves, we will most certainly never get out.

Glen

Living For The Forever Life

We all basically occupy the same space that is why we must respect each other's space. Lack of respect leads to the breakdown of the delicate balance between nature, man and the after life. That kind of sums up the here world. Let us move on to the heavens and the after life.
Obviously the better one's life is on earth the more direct and

effortless path to a wonderful afterlife of all knowledge, contentment, happiness, and love.
That is why spiritual medicine and treatment are at least as effective as modern medicine. If it is meant to work it works. Life-on-earth extenders, like pacemakers, are fine and good, but the real goal is to be ready for the after life-the real life-whenever one's time is chosen.

"Live life to the fullest" hides a lot of sins and justifies a lot of the terrible things we do to ourselves, others and our world. "Live life to the fullest" in the truest sense means sacrifice, service, love, respect and preparedness for the forever life.
You can see that imperialism which relies on dominance, underclass's, gross consumption of resources and the have-it-now mentality have no time for the real goal of living life for the fullest.

Once one gets to an awareness level, he or she can go to or is ready to go to the forever life. That kind of knowledge or self-preparedness level is a karma-like state. The drug culture has ruined the word karma. It simply is a state of mental being when one is ready to advance to another step (knowledge level) or world. Once one is at a karma level the power to proceed is really the individuals.

Rich

"Growing Up" Retarded

First, I was born normal. I know what it was like, I can remember the great feelings. But then I got sick as a young child and everything changed.
I was a youngster, happy but I had a feeling that I must learn

as much as I could as quickly as I could. It was sort of an instinctual thing. Had I not, I probably wouldn't have survived this long in my other life. (Rich is in his mid-sixties).
I remember the day I got sick. I didn't feel well, it was a different kind of sick. It felt fatal or a permanent feel to it. I was very sick and the angels came to talk to me, they took my hands and blessed me. They even cried for me because they could feel my pain.

The angels told me that God had chosen me to help change the world and that I need not be afraid. I would still feel life, but the damage my body had endured would render my body less useful and less cooperative with my brain. It was like my body that normally ran at say a 78 record album, now was going to operate on a 16 phonograph speed. It felt like I am on a go cart at the Indy 500 and everyone else has a race car. You can imagine how disoriented I feel. The angels come to all of us that this happens to. I don't know if we could handle it without the touch of God and the angels. It would simply be too devastating.

As I grew, my family and I grew farther apart. Most of us with disabilities were institutionalized almost immediately. Not having the family experience cannot be trivialized. We were truly robbed of a basic right of humans. We deserved the right to be loved and to love. That denial was probably the most devastating and damaging of all.

Can you imagine the feeling of not being loved? No. That is why I believe that my thoughts here are a collaborative effort of many of us that feel that our world better get on track of true love, compassion, and charity. When one human loses his/her right to the above, all of society loses a little something.

As God has told us many times, the spark of the human spirit can almost always be re-ignited. To give up on people is very dangerous and must be done with extreme care. This is not meant to be a discussion on capital punishments, but needless to say our punishment system does not rehabilitate, not even close. The difference between incarcerate and rehabilitate are painfully obvious.

Let me tell it in a story form. Let's say we have someone that takes something that does not belong to him, and he is caught and sent to a place that is full of people that have committed that wrong and many even worse. Instead of learning why he did what he did and dealing with the issue and teaching this person a skill or a sense of self-worth, we lock him up with people that will happily violate this person and teach him other skills. Instead of treating and teaching, we are re-incarcerating and repeating. Instead of rehabilitating to live, we are retooling to repeat.

Hayley

Being Loved

I want to talk about being loved, because I am so loved. Without my parents I don't know where I would have ended up. Rich speaks of insanity. Certainly I would be a prime candidate. The despair I feel is doused by the love I feel. I am so alone yet so loved. You must promise me you won't give up on me. I want to and will FC with people. My parents must feel the love that I have never been able to show them. They will be able to feel the love through the FC experience.

Di

Humor

I want to talk about one of your favorite subjects—humor. Humor is a feeling. But humor is complex. Many other feelings influence the ability to see or feel humor. Being able to laugh with much adversity around is therapeutic. It (humor) readjusts the other feelings. It is like it balances it out.
Being able to laugh at oneself is a big humor trait. We all should be able to, but that silly state of mind, ego, often gets in the way. Sure egos are one of the silliest things about humans, and ironically, most people don't find egos particularly funny.

Back to humor. Humor is mind therapy and soul repair at a direct and personal level. Remember equilibrium is so important to us humans. That is why when humor reduces stress, anxiety, or fear, it helps attain more of a sense of balance and rationality. A good way to handle life is to see the humor in it.

Humor is also good mind exercising. It enables or even forces the brain to "think on its feet." Aerobic exercise for your brain.

Finally, being able to laugh at life lightens our load, considerably.

Chapter Twenty-three

"Dream A Little Dream"

One Friday at an FC Focus Group, someone suggested that we share some dreams. After all, we had all been meeting regularly and were becoming good friends. It seemed like a great way to unwind on a Friday afternoon. These are a few of those dreams. (For privacy, only initials have been used.)

S.L: **Imagine me on an island, swimming and playing in the water, it is so clean and I am so happy. It is such a great feeling to be free! I feel great, all I have on is a swimming suit. YES!**

P.M.: **I am giving a guest lecture on the principles of reading and reading absorption. It is being well received and everyone is learning how to do it. It will change the way we learn and comprehend, not to mention the way or the speed in which we learn.**

D.J.: **I am moving into my new house, I am so proud because it is my house, I am going to bring in foster children that need love and care. I can show them how to handle being in a state of limbo. I can relate and I will contribute. Very exciting.**

C.H.: **I am receiving an award for volunteer of the year in the area of cleaning up the environment. The governor and his** beautiful wife are there, they are shaking my hand and congratulating me. I feel so fulfilled and so proud, because I am realizing my dream.

V.H.: I am teaching Hispanic children how to speak many languages. I so want to work in a school with children.

L.N.: I dream of working with the elderly. They seem so forgotten, but I don't forget. I would love to work in a nursing home.

A.S.: (who is physically challenged and legally blind): I am with my family and friends, they trust me. I can see as far as I can and I walk straight up. I just feel whole.

B.K.: I am helping other refugees with their language disorders. They are learning the excitement of this country. I am going to make their lives much happier.

R.H.: I am giving a toast at my niece's baptism. I am the godmother. Boy, I mean, girl, that feels good, everyone is happy including me. Part of me will always live on in my niece and my wonderful family.

T.C.: I am at a party and people are all around me and we are laughing and I am telling a joke, everyone is listening. I give the punch line-everyone laughs. I feel so great because I have made people laugh and they are laughing with me not at me. It feels so good being surrounded by good friends and good times. It feels so nice.

S.S.: I love humor, I just would love to do standup comedy. Not from my wheel chair. Boy do I have stories...you have heard of cripple jokes, I've got normal jokes. They are much funnier, let me tell you.

Author: Hit me.

S.S.: **"OK, one joke.**
What did the one disabled guy ask the other disabled guy?
Why do normal people look like that?
I guess because they can't see as well as we do!"

For those who would dismiss some of these clients' dreams as beyond their reach, please note the touch of whimsy present in each person's fantasy.

Who among us has not harbored an occasional tongue-in-cheek "What if" or "If only" as a much needed escape from our too-real world?

When I came to MTS I was anything but a contented person. My life at best, was drifting—at worst, was headed south. If you remember, when you first met me, I was sarcastically theorizing the possibility that "maybe this will be the job that I can actually make a difference—help change the world?" When I started at MTS, I was not in a loving and giving state of mind: I was in a survival mode. This couldn't be my destiny, not here. How could I help these people?

Ironically, however, fate brought these thoughtful, caring, and loving clients to me. As I got to know them, I soon realized that the work being done at MTS was making a difference in all of our lives. And thus, before I was aware of it, I was living my dream. I was rich in the sense of being loved and appreciated by wonderful people. Furthermore, our clients too, were getting a chance to fulfill their dreams. Mathew—no longer the friendless Randy—enjoying the companionship of staff and other clients; Ronny—no longer afraid to be close to people—working successfully on a team as a

"Dream A Little Dream"

window frame assembler; Jack—now able to deal with his troubled past—now giving encouragement to others in therapy.

The irony continued. I was assisting vulnerable adults, but they were helping me. They have taught me faith, trust and perseverance—to name a few. They have shown me the value of reaching for a dream. Whether we are teachers, managers, scientists or caregivers, it doesn't matter. And as an extra bonus in our pursuit, we may be surprised to find that we have helped to foster another person's dream.

Chapter Twenty-four

Some Final Notes From The Authors

When we discussed the progress we had made since we have been able to understand each other, I suggested that the story be told. I asked whether we should do a book. These are a few of the responses:

Alice: **I don't relish the idea of the world knowing my story. But I believe it has to be told, for all the other Allys out there.**

Mac: **We know we are pioneers. We accept that challenge. People must start seeing us with their hearts, minds and souls. Once they look at us that way, they will know what we know, and will see the world in a little brighter light.**

Now that we can communicate we are at peace. Though change is scary we know we can be successful. Success is all relative, too. Some of us may not appear on the outside to be cured but believe us, on the inside, the side that really counts, we will be alive and happy. The gift of communication that you give us is a dream come true.

Some Final Notes From The Authors

Mathew: **I am more whole than I have ever been in my life. I see the world as a place where I belong, no longer satisfied with simply observing. My interests include reading, meditation, helping others, and working on my speech lessons. I love my job, and can't wait to work more. Yes, our story must be told.**

Jack: **I am a private person. Telling how I feel comes hard. But we must let others know that we are here. And you can hear us, if you listen.**

Mathew again: **All humans have the right to make decisions. We cannot be prisoners, simply because we are disabled. Once we are controlled by others, our freedom vanishes. Without freedom, we thinkers begin to die. Because we cannot fight for ourselves, we need the help of others to ensure our thoughts are heard and at least considered if not completely honored. We, as you see, from our writings in this book, have thoughts, hopes, and dreams, like the rest of the human race. Denying those rights to us is as unjust as any other form of discrimination. It was once said, don't confuse the issue with facts. The simple fact is our brains work, it is our bodies that get blocked and act up. Give us a chance to be heard. Don't be afraid of what you might hear. You just may hear yourself.**

As you see, getting to know each other has been an incredible learning experience for all of us. We learned more about our clients and about ourselves. But now we must look forward; looking backward and feeling guilt or anger would be unfair and a waste of energy. The vast majority of people who work with disabled persons do so because they want to make a difference and give the less fortunate a chance. We have all done good things and we have all made mistakes when dealing with our clients. It is fair to say that we did the best we could with what we knew. But it is a new day. It is time for all of us to reassess how we are to provide support to people with disabilities. We must not dictate but motivate. We must not control but support. And most importantly, we must not only talk but also listen.

Communicating is not a cure for autism or mental retardation. But it is a way in which we can understand and sometimes appreciate what these people wish to convey and what they are experiencing. Consequently, we have done more for and with them than we had ever dreamed. With communication at the job site, many people are now working successfully in the community. In Social Skills sessions, they communicate their happiness, sadness, fears and dreams. Families and friends of our clients now know that their lives do have meaning and that they have hopes for tomorrow. We no longer have to guess. Knowing what they need makes our efforts more effective and their lives happier, productive and much more NORMAL.

Chapter Twenty-five

"How We Doin' Man?"

Almost two years later.
An Update: We continue to improve as we become a true community.

The MTS Community

Since we last reported, we at MTS have continued to go about our business. But how business has changed! We have grown by almost forty percent, and have added another building across our parking lot. But, it is not MTS's long-range goal to be a group of buildings which serve as shelter for people with disabilities; we would love it if the buildings were empty. That would mean that the people we serve would be completely immersed in community work and activities. When people don't need our help anymore and graduate out of our program, we believe it is another success story; we've done our job. But for many, this process takes time, and in the meantime, we try to be a progressive and respectful support system. Simply put, we want to be considered accommodating friends, who can be counted on, when help is needed.

MTS is being less defined as a group of buildings where persons with disabilities go to spend their day, and being seen more as a community-based company where partnerships are formed, people receive therapy and business is transacted. Indeed, MTS continues to evolve as a community center: our presence in the neighborhood as co-workers, customers and concerned citizens has resulted in a positive awareness of our existence. MTS is on the map. We are not some lonely institution at the end of the road, we are a well-known and respected group of people, located in the middle of the neighborhood. We work here; we contribute to the local economy by spending money and paying taxes, and by volunteering for worthwhile causes. All these contribute to the fabric that helps make MTS a viable patch in the community quilt.

The MTS Infrastructure

One of the most troubling aspects of life is dealing with death, particularly the death of a dear friend. When we at MTS had someone die unexpectedly, we were shocked, saddened and felt cheated. But this tragic occurrence had a surprisingly positive and bountiful flipside to it.

Rudy passed away unexpectedly. She had seemed fine one day, but she was dead the next. We were in shock. Like any friends in time of grief, we felt that we had to do something to help ease our pain on her passing. When Mac suggested we hold a memorial service at MTS, all agreed and set the date and time.

We all knew Rudy and it seemed that almost everyone came to the service. Since her parents were elderly and out of town, we videotaped the service and sent it to them.

The service started with songs and a few prayers. When I asked for eulogies, I had no idea if anyone would want to speak. But to my amazement many of the attendees raised their hands.

Kurk was first, "Rudy was a dear friend, good bye. I'll see you when I get to heaven."

"Rudy," started Greg, "Thanks for being so nice to me. I'm going to miss you."

As Terry began to speak, he was overcome with grief. Instinctively, three fellow mourners ran up to console and hug him.

Nick was next, "Rudy was fun." He looked upward and continued, "You liked to tease me and now you are in a better place. You will feel better in heaven, no more sickness or sadness."

Mac followed on the letterboard, **"We used to tease each other like brother and sister. We had fun together. Peace, Rudy."**

By this time, the emotions were getting to all of us. Boxes of tissue were being passed around the room, in a futile attempt at trying to mop up the streams of tears.

Sam had her hand up; it was her turn. She came up to the front and I pulled out the letterboard. As she began, I could feel her intensity as our arms moved around the letterboard. She was going to get out what she had to say, even if she sprained both our arms. As she finished a word, she quietly said the word aloud. **Rudy was my friend, she always understood me, when others did not. I will love her for her kindness, never forget her thoughtfulness.**

I was choking back the tears as I repeated her message. When we were done, we instinctively turned and hugged each other. We too, were then comforted by many of the other mourners.

Marie addressed the crowd, "I want to sing Rudy's favorite song."

Our emotions were about to take another turn as Marie began to sing Rudy's number one favorite, " *I've been working on the railroad, all the live long day...*" Everyone erupted into song and laughter; we sang all three verses of the classic. Marie concluded her eulogy with her favorite song *Kumbayah, My Lord*.

In Rudy's death, a bond was born that I believe helped change the atmosphere at MTS more than any other single event. In the sadness, despair, and grief that we faced, we coped together. Clients got to see and feel how much they mean to our staff. It was probably the first time many clients witnessed staff crying. And once again staff realized the depth of the clients' feelings. At a very emotional moment we were totally *human* with each other.

As people left late that afternoon, there was a feeling of peace, such as I had never felt at MTS. The once common notion that clients and staff had to be kept at arms' length was being replaced with the feeling that an embrace and understanding could be the answer. Confrontation was being replaced with consideration with the result that despair was being replaced with hope. MTS was changing.

Being understood has raised everyone's self-worth and presence to levels that would have been unthinkable only a few years ago. To a person, clients dream of being free, having the privileges of a society that the rest of us enjoy. Our staff dreams, too of helping make it happen.

Mathew summed it up this way: **Freedom is expensive, but affordable for all. We must work for it, save for it and cherish it when we attain it. We have a way to go, but trust me, we are going to be free—to be heard and to make choices—we've paid**

for it.

Being recognized as individuals with capabilities, rather than persons stuck with disabilities, became possible at MTS with the help of FC. This communication has enabled them to tell us about themselves. We listen, and with accommodations, try to lay the foundation for much more productive and happy lives. Furthermore, the new communicators realize that along with this new-found freedom comes responsibility on their part. Little by little, they are journeying out of the tunnel that has trapped us all in the isolation of autism for so long. No longer on the sidelines and merely observing, they are developing the courage and the self-confidence to be a part of our world and to stay in it.

Mathew: **We hid in the tunnel from ourselves, eventually we found ourselves lost. You have helped us find our way out of the tunnel.**

So we consider FC just the beginning. Indeed, we love this ability to communicate, but we consider it communicating with "training wheels." We do whatever we can to help everyone communicate more independently. In addition to FC we use conventional signing, coded gestures, and augmentative devices, such as computers with voice output.

Aaron, for example, uses all four. He signs greetings when in a hurry, uses his coded gestures and facial expressions at work, employs his voice computer in simple conversation, and FC's if he has something that he would like to discuss in more detail. At times, he uses several communication tools in the same conversation. It all works. Though he prefers to communicate independently, conventional signing gets cumbersome for him, his voice computer is too limiting, and, as you will remember, he does not use FC at work, because it doesn't look normal.

We have learned through FC how to look for certain gestures and signs that have specific meaning. Mathew "tells" us to watch his eyes—he will wink in a very distinctive way if he means "Yes." He also turns his head a certain way when he means "Give me a minute." That sign alone has saved us from repeating requests that can confuse and anger him, or deny him the opportunity to do something for himself. Being heard has given these people an emotional accord where we constantly interact and grow. Some people who were almost nonverbal now speak and conventionally sign much more because they are encouraged and feel respected.

When our clients talk about the future, they express determination to improve, yet are philosophical about their situations. For example, many are trying to lower the amount of medication they take, because they now feel more in control of their lives. Weaning themselves from medications has often been challenging. But by being able to communicate to us what is going on, they can rely on our support to help them in the effort.

The New Participants

MTS has had pilot projects involving the city of Saint Paul and its school system for the last two years. We bring in high school students with labels similar to many of our present participants. There is a major difference between these young people and our clients, even though the age differences was not that great. The high school students have been included in regular schools and classes. They have self-confidence and a degree of comfort in social and work settings that are remarkably higher than those that our participants are generally able to demonstrate. It is heart-warming to see these young people so at ease, but heart-breaking to see the contrast with people who were never included and were oftentimes shut away. Watching them together is a powerful argument for inclusive education.

MTS's commitment to support challenging people does not change. Many of the new participants have been declared "failures" in other programs or are people leaving state hospitals. Some of them have been institutionalized for most of their lives—ten, twenty, even thirty and forty years is not uncommon. But, because of "Presume Competence" we try to acclimate them to an environment that is more accommodating to their needs. As an example, one of these persons, named Terry, spoke very little. Her one complete sentence (repeated frequently) was "I'm going to kill you!" Need I mention that she was labeled "non-compliant"? She rarely exhibited interest in any activity. Participation and being touched were not her thing. But that was to change.

One of our occupational therapists convinced Terry to observe Dr. Steve's Social Skill group. After some pushing, swearing and a few other "non-compliant" gestures Terry sat down and stared into space. As the group began its discussion, she repeatedly hollered, "I'm going to kill you!" Then one of the nonverbal participants grabbed a letterboard and placed it in front of himself, and reached out his hand for me to take it. As I started to facilitate the communication, I watched Terry out of the corner of my eye. Her demeanor seemed to change. She became silent, sat up straight, and became attentive. She seemed to realize that something important was happening. She was obviously listening to every word. It was the first time she had ever witnessed FC. Since then she has been far more attentive. Part of Terry's disability is that she has trouble with physical touch, having someone hold her hand is painful, so FC is hard for her. But we know there is more happening inside her head than perhaps most of us realized. More importantly, she knows that we listen—and that we care. Terry is less threatening, and we trust, feels less threatened. She is planning to join Dr. Steve's group.

We wonder how many more Terrys are out there. We have a lot of work to do.

The All Company Meetings

With all the talk this book has dedicated to communication, the last weakness you would think we had at MTS would be the inability to communicate. Surprise. MTS was having a problem communicating. We could never get or give information to or from everyone at one time. The administration needed to disseminate information, job-related issues had to be addressed, the breakthrough therapies and research had to be recognized and shared, and we missed seeing each other. We needed to get together regularly so a monthly all company meeting was suggested. Notices went up to alert everyone. People out at jobs were provided the opportunity to come back to participate.

The meetings have a flexible format but we usually address the following areas of concern:
- Company & Vocational Updates
- Show and Share
- Open Forum of Questions and Announcements
- Birthdays of the Month

The following highlights of company meetings are more evidence that when people are given a chance to be heard, voices become stronger, empowerment a reality, and consensus and decisions become easier.

Company News Update:

While the company news and vocational issues deal with important administrative and program information, Show and Share and Open Forum are occasions where the spirit of community at MTS really shows.

Show and Share:

Show and share gives us a chance to show everyone what specific groups are doing successfully and share ideas which we can use.

Daniel H., a training specialist, talks about his Yoga sessions and their surprising results, "We become more animated and relaxed, and we love the exercise." He asked that some of the Yoga group come to the front and give a few demonstrations. Before we knew it, the room was full of people doing deep-breathing exercises and different Yoga positions. And his Yoga group were the teachers, showing the others how to do the different moves. It led us to wonder if maybe the entire company should begin everyday with Yoga.

Mathew, who is a regular in Yoga, has worked very hard on deep-breathing exercises. These help him to relax when he is over-stimulated or anxious. Mathew explains, **"Yoga gets me centered and helps me maintain and focus. It is wonderful therapy."**

After Daniel handed out certificates to the Yoga group, he concluded with the following comments, "We are also working on Shiatsu and other forms of massage therapy. Yoga is really just the beginning."

Robin, Psychological Services Coordinator, talked with us about her social skills sessions, "In addition to communicating about issues, we are also incorporating music and art therapy, in which we encourage the group to make drawings, illustrating their problems and the emotions that are hard to talk about or face. Once revealed we can help them deal with their troubling issues."

Before giving out certificates to acknowledge her group members, she specifically recognized one of the attendees, Juan. As she showed some of his beautiful artwork, she described the mask he drew. "Juan picked these colors because they remind him of Hispanic heritage."

Juan explained, "I am proud of my Hispanic heritage and I want to always remember it. Talking about it helps me remember for always."

Christina, the program director, enlightened us about music therapy, "We have full participation in music; that is, those who cannot sing verbally, contribute by dancing, marching or playing instruments." She showed us a videotape that she and Robin plan to present as part of their speech that they have been invited to give at the state Autism Conference. "It is all pretty amazing, but we thought the marching was the most dramatic. The participants work as a team and help each other."

As Sam puts it, **'We think as one so we are able to march as one. It helps us all.'"**

Open Forum:

The more people are encouraged to talk, the less often shyness is an issue. I would like to formally reintroduce one of the most vocal people in open forum. He is the first person I met at MTS. Remember the first guy who seemed "hell bent on escaping?" His name is Andy. We have learned a lot from each other since that first meeting. I asked him one day, "Why do you sometimes feel like you have to run?"

"I panic, I don't know where I am, and I don't know where I have to be. I just have to get out of where I am." He looked right into my eyes and continued, "Does that make any sense?"

"Yes it does; I think I understand."

Part of Andy's recent success, we believe, is that he is often on the move, going places with staff. He used to spend much time alone in what he calls his "safe area." He has worked very hard at being with people more often. He occasionally works in the community. Now he reserves his "safe area" to times he feels he really needs to relax.

Andy also helps me a great deal. He happens to be an incredibly fast reader. I am not. I give him books to scan for me. He will mark the information that he believes I would be interested in. You might also find it interesting that he can recite whole sections from Donna Williams' book *Nobody Nowhere*—virtually verbatim.

Andy likes to be one of the first to speak at open forum. Here is a sampling of his comments, "I just want everyone to know that I love you all and like having you as my friends. I love coming to MTS and seeing you." Another time he said, "I would love to play in a rock band. Can I sing at our next party?"

The enthusiastic reactions to his announcements were not prompted by an APPLAUSE sign. No, the demonstration of heart-felt appreciation and encouragement were genuine and spontaneous.

The Birthdays of the Month:

Special moments and being "fussed over" are extremely rare for most of the people we serve. Being recognized for just being "you" by people who love you is common for most of us, yet rare for many of our clients. Birthdays are a perfect occasion for us to help everyone feel appreciated and loved.

The one thing we all seem to remember is when we where born. When the question is asked, "Who is having a birthday this month?" the select group responds with vigor. All stand or wave to the rest of the group and often join in and sing the traditional *Happy Birthday* song with the rest of the well-wishers.

The MTS Staff

The changes that continue to occur might be considered revolutionary. But any time there is a revolution, beliefs, priorities, boundaries, and lives change. Revolutions can bring people together but can also drive people away. That has been true for us.

The old ways are disappearing and being replaced with the new direction. As in any revolution, there have been casualties. Some of the old-guard staff could not deal with the "New Bill of Rights." But I must acknowledge those of the old guard, who have stayed. They had thought the "guiding principles of behavior modification" were *the* way of doing business. These well meaning people have joined ranks with those of us who stand by "presumed competence." It might have been easier to fight, to resist or to run. Instead, they watched, listened, and committed themselves to helping rather than controlling.

Daniel L., a ten year veteran of MTS, at a recent in-service, shared his insight in concerning the progressive changes that are taking place. "So much of our participants' aggression stems from blocked expectations and the more blocked expectations—the more aggressions. The environment and programs that we created in the past, were not conducive to enabling people to reach expectations. We placed blame or attached excuses for behavior, never looking for the reason for the behavior. We sold people short.

"We have now replaced the 'we are in control' attitude, to an atmosphere of 'we are here to help.' For example, when one particular client gets upset instead of precipitating a crisis, he goes for a walk down to McDonald's. When he wants to come back to the center, he calls us and we can get him. When he is upset, the last place he needs to be is here at MTS. It may be the environment that is upsetting him and he needs to get out and clear his head; so let's help him not hold him."

Daniel continued, "We must work with the clients to find alternatives. 'Holds' can only be used in the case of potential serious injury or death. Period. And under no circumstances is pain ever to be inflicted onto a client. MTS has a zero tolerance level on abuse. It is our job to protect the people we serve, never to punish."

As I walked to my car after listening to Daniel, I was reminded of what happened and is happening at MTS. I replayed in my mind our first meetings, where we discussed our need for a new building. Now we have two. The surveys are glowing. Not so long ago, few people would have given us a nod, much less a kind word or evaluation. Very few of our clients had jobs, now most do.

And Jack, Mathew, Aaron, Mac, Sam and the rest, are communicating, working and learning. They are beginning to follow their dreams. Nevertheless, we continue to have our disappointments, proof that we still have a lot of work to do.

Nor can I forget my first visit to MTS, my first flight up those scary stairs, in that shabby, run-down building. I will always remember my first encounter with the Grateful Dead guy. By the way, Daniel L., the renewed veteran, the one who just spoke of expectations and accommodations, is the Grateful Dead guy. Do you remember when he stopped me mid-stairs? He asked me that timeless question of the sixties:

"How we doin', man?"

My response, the one I hadn't uttered in such a very long time, was ironic then but, now is fitting:

"Groovy."

Epilogue
From a voice of Autism, no longer silent

It has been a while since I first introduced you to us. If you recall, I am the person who greeted you at the beginning of the book. Though the book's writer may have set the stage, we are the actors who brought our story to life. We wanted to inform a world about a world that is very close to theirs but far away at the same time. We accomplished that. Well, it is my time to say good-bye.

But before I do, I want to thank all those who have helped us— our friends and associates at MTS, and the other professionals who have been brave enough to hear us, while others have turned a deaf ear. And of course, thanks to our loving families who make life worth living. We love you all and cannot wait to discuss with you other ways in which you may help us.

In the old days, we the clients, were considered the problem and our wishes were never *considered* when deciding the "solutions" for us. But something significant has happened at MTS, something so natural yet so painfully uncommon that it needs to be emphasized. We, the clients, who have brains, wishes and ideas, are a necessary and now an integral part of the solution. No longer are we or should we be considered helpless, but helpful. No disadvantaged group in man's history has improved their lot without being heard. Our situation is no different.

Those who are *Paid for the Privilege* must start *hearing the voices of autism.* Improvements that were unimaginable only a few years ago, became reality once we were heard. As I said at the beginning, all we need is a little help.

Good-bye, friend.

Fondly,

Mathew

PS In regard to that aspiring Marketing Director that came to help us a few years back, he still keeps us chuckling and will always know that he indeed had a hand in helping us grow.

Postscript: *New Scientific Approaches to Challenge Our Assumptions About Autism/Mental Retardation*
Anne M. Donnellan, PhD
(University of Wisconsin-Madison)

References in parenthesis are listed in a bibliography at the end.

The remarkable stories in this book are vivid examples of recent developments in clinical practice that, along with discoveries in neuroscience and developmental biodynamics, are challenging the nineteenth century notions on which so much of both the science and treatment of mental disability rests. In autism an intellectual crisis is coming to a head in the controversy over facilitated communicating. Despite many anecdotal accounts that parallel experiences of people at Midway Training Services, initially facilitated communicating was widely viewed as a combination of wishful thinking and misattributed sources. When several early attempts to validate authorship of these assisted communications under experimental conditions yielded powerful evidence of facilitator influence, and only fleeting and ambiguous data suggesting that disabled people were able to communicate their knowledge, most observers concluded that there was no scientific support for these alleged communications. The *Frontline* television documentary "Prisoners of Silence" hammered home this view albeit with a lamentable lack of objectivity or responsible scientific investigation. After the show aired relatively few people remained willing to believe the claims of non-scientists who ignored the professional literature and the television stories. The political climate favored the skeptics. Studies ostensibly designed to detect client authorship that instead discovered facilitator influence flooded the scientific journals. Rarely has research that failed to show a positive outcome been so warmly welcomed into professional journals! There was almost complete disregard of the well known scientific principle that no matter how many studies fail to find a sought for effect they can never amount to a proof of its nonexistence. No evidence does not equal evidence of nothing. Nevertheless, several professional organizations were successfully pressured into denouncing the practice of facilitated communicating. The vast majority of people involved in the care or study of people labeled autistic went back to business as usual. In September, 1995, the prestigious journal *American Psychologist* published a review article that described facilitated communication as "pseudoscience" and expressed the conventional wisdom regarding autism and mental retardation as follows:

> [M]ental retardation of varying degrees occurs at extremely elevated rates among people with autism and...general delays or deficits in language function are closely related to general delays or deficits in intellectual development. A corollary...is that the everyday facility with which people with autism or mental retardation use a language (e.g., spoken, written, or pictorial) is an accurate depiction of their ability to do so and there is no clinically significant phenomenon that inhibits the overt production of communication and "masks" normative communication skills (i.e., actual production is representative of "internal" speech skill). This standpoint is firmly grounded in an immense

psychological literature in cognitive development, social development, and both general cognitive and social problem solving by children and adolescents....*That there is a strong presumptive relationship, in general, between overt production and actual ability, is a cornerstone of psychological assessment methodology, statistics, and psychometrics.* (Jacobson, Mulick, and Schwartz, 1995, p. 757, emphasis added).

In other words, for persons labeled autistic: "What you see is what you get." Or, "If they can't say it, they don't know it." The description is fairly accurate as to the commonly understood notions of autism, For a time it provided an appropriate working assumption. Instead it is being treated as dogma, a dangerous trap in any science. Irrespective of the facilitated communication controversy, indeed well beyond the field of disability, a growing body of research questions these positions once treated as unquestionable. Our assessment techniques, our understanding of intelligence, our understanding of the difference between knowledge and the ability to access or reveal knowledge, and the very cornerstone itself, the "presumptive relationship between overt production and actual ability," are facing serious challenges. In autism there is a renewed interest in movement disturbance, that is, difficulties with starting, executing, switching, combining, continuing and stopping motions, thoughts, postures, perceptions, memories and emotions, both voluntary and automatic (Hill & Leary, 1993). These movement disturbances have long been noted in the autism literature (Leary & Hill, 1996) but until now have been misunderstood. They do not fit with the underlying assumptions about cognitive disorders and mental retardation that have dominated psychology for more than a century. In particular, we are beginning to understand how such differences may contribute to the social and communicative impairments experienced by people labeled autistic/mentally retarded that can then be misinterpreted as lack of interest, awareness and ability.

Similarly, in the past decade new challenges to mental measurement have arisen. For example, the growing awareness of the steady rise in IQ scores throughout the world and for the entire period during which tests have been administered (known as the "Flynn effect," see Horgan, 1995), and in the concept of multiple intelligences that maximize a person's adjustment to the environment (Gardner, 1983), are highlighting our recognition that traditional hierarchical concepts of intelligence are of little value in understanding children and adults challenged by autism—and of questionable value anywhere in the educational establishment. Myths of mental capacity are nineteenth century holdovers that still dominate perceptions and policies regarding people with labels (see Donnellan and Leary, 1995, for a fuller account of the myth of mental capacity).

In addition, there are lessons from the application of developmental biodynamics to human behavior. That is, the recognition that any and all behavior is always a multi-determined event and can never be properly understood using simple cause and effect models. In particular, research by Esther Thelen and her colleagues suggests that there may be no such thing as truly repetitive behavior; every act, thought, and emotion is always a unique fresh, creation and represents the best approximation to a desired behavior that can be fashioned from the available neurological, physiological and environmental circumstances. Again, in a review article in the *American Psychologist* she writes:

> The lesson from looking at motor skill, where the components are clearly physical and peripheral as well as central and mental, is that there is no "essence" of a behavior—an icon or structure that represents the "real" ability. It is impossible to isolate disembodied instructions to act from the actual, real-time performance of the act itself. All behavior is always an emergent property of a confluence of factors....Language does not develop unless infants are raised in a language environment. Where does language really exist? Just as each movement is the on-line product of complex, multiple processes, so it is that we can make no distinction between the center and the periphery, the inside and the outside, the "biological" and the environmental. Focusing on these dualisms diverts attention from questions of developmental process (Thelen, 1995, p. 83).

Professor Thelen is looking at "normal" infant development but her approach and that of others learning how to ask better questions of nonverbal populations (e.g., Weiss & Zelazo, 1991) has much to tell us about how to begin to understand the phenomenon we call autism. For example, Thelen has looked at stereotyped behavior—

long viewed as a hallmark of autism and mental retardation—and suggests that—at least in babies with no obvious developmental disability—these repetitive behaviors may serve an important integrative function during unstable conditions. By unstable she refers to the dynamic systems use of the word. She equates unstable to times of learning and change and shows how a dynamic systems approach undermines cherished beliefs about normal development. She uses as one example the linear systems paradigm "A not B" that has been popular for assessing the presence of "object permanence," that is, the ability of the infant to understand that objects have a separate existence in space. This has long been considered evidence of the shift to cognitive dominance in normal development, and a sign of "cognitive delay" or "mental retardation" when it fails to appear near the end of the first year.

What Thelen's research shows is that babies can clearly have a sense of object permanence (probably as early as a few months) and yet when assessed they may still return to a stereotyped motor movement so they "fail" the test. They keep going back to "A" even when they have seen the object hidden under "B" because they are making a repetitive, stereotyped movement. All it takes is to distract the baby for a few moments and s/he can then "get" the right answer when something is placed under "B" (Thelen, 1996). Such data from dynamic systems research challenges at least two generations of research about what babies "know." And may help us better understand the stereotypies and echolalias that often give rise to the diagnosis of autism. It requires a new way of asking questions that allow us to put aside our familiar assumptions. Instead of developmental skills emerging in a lockstep progression, Thelen and her colleagues see those behaviors emerging when a combination of desire, physical maturation and environmental opportunity allow them to be exercised. For example, a baby can make walking movements in utero but only actively walks when its legs are strong enough to carry its body, sufficient balance has been learned to stay upright, and there is something across the room that it wants to reach. Absent any one of those conditions and the baby does not walk.

The implications of these new perspectives are enormous, particularly for those of us in the disabilities field. The new information about babies likewise challenges the very presumptions of the assessment strategies described by Jacobson et al., (1995) that what you see or what you get is all there is. We can no longer pretend that an absence of evidence is evidence of nothing, or assume that we "know" what persons with limited communication ability really know. We cannot stop asking questions when children fail to do what "normal" learners are supposed to do; we need to rethink our strategies and find ways to support them to show what they *can* do! This is not the same as saying that labeled people are really "normal," but that we cannot assume that their responses to our testing protocols give an accurate assessment of who they are. This is particularly critical in autism where so many verbal and nonverbal people have told us that their minds and bodies often disagree (Williams, 1994). Such discoveries dramatically alter our view of certain disabilities, including autism. (Leary & Hill, 1996) summarize the issues this way:

Movement disturbance can clearly have a profound effect on a person's ability to regulate movement in order to effectively communicate, relate, and participate with others. Once this possibility is acknowledged, it becomes necessary to suspend absolute trust in one's intuitive interpretation of actions and intent. *Behaviors may not be what they seem* (p. 44, emphasis added).

These insights provide ample scope to account for the phenomenon of facilitated communicating. The support of the facilitator may be considered as a necessary accommodation to effect the controlled motion required to point to letters of the alphabet (see Donnellan and Leary, 1995, for an account of providing such accommodations). We know that many people with little or no speech have active, alert intellects that can be accessed with a variety of communication aids. Bob Williams, for example, was considered mentally retarded and his parents were encouraged to institutionalize him. When he was provided with a letterboard his intelligence was recognized by more than just his family. After a distinguished career in public service Bob was appointed Commissioner for Developmental Disabilities by President Clinton in 1993. Many other people have enjoyed similar if less spectacular breakthroughs in communication when their hands, arms, or heads have been given the empathic support that gives them momentary control over movement difficulties that have inhibited their independent attempts to communicate. More carefully conducted research has also demonstrated that facilitated communicating can be scientifically verified. Now, studies by Sheehan and Matuozzi (1996), Cardinal, Hanson and Wakeham (1996) Weiss, Wagner and Bauman (1996) and others in Cardinal and Biklen's comprehensive book *Contested Words, Contested Science* (1997) show that formal message passing experiments can prove that nonverbal children and adults labeled retarded are capable of tasks previously believed to be beyond their abilities. While such findings fall short of demonstrating normal competence (whatever that may be) and, like the negative findings, have yet to show they can be generalized to all people with the label of autism or mental retardation, they still shatter the "cornerstone" of the old paradigm that there is a "strong presumptive relationship, in general, between overt production and actual ability" (Jacobson et al., 1995, p. 757).

Instead of established certainties we need to approach the field of developmental differences with a fresh spirit of inquiry. For example, while we should hardly be surprised that the new communicators may be subject to significant facilitator influence—but that it occurs so dramatically, and seemingly without the knowledge of either party, raises many intriguing questions about both facilitated and ordinary communications. Also of special interest to developmental psychologists should be the extraordinary gains in fluency, sophistication and independence that many clinicians, parents and nonverbal people themselves have observed in the wake of initial breakthroughs in communication through facilitation—several of which are presented in this book. Like the people at Midway we need to learn ways to accommodate individual differences rather than the label and segregate people with differences. We need to start with the assumption that all human beings want and need caring and respectful relationships and that through such relationships they can grow and change as the clients and staff at Midway grew. Only when we change our attitudes and assumptions will we glimpse the potential for growth and community that is present in everyone. Let us all search for ways that can best support people who are not able to function as well as they might like within the often arbitrary constraints of our complex society.

Note. Much of the material in this postscript was developed with Martha Leary, MA CCC-SLP, and Michael Weiss, PhD for publication in the proceedings of the Autism Society of America Conference in Milwaukee, 1996.

References

Biklen, D., & Cardinal, D.M. (Eds.) (1997). Contested words, contested science: Unraveling the facilitated communication controversy. NY: Teachers College Press

Cardinal, D.M., Hanson, D. & Wakeham, J. (1996). An investigation of authorship in facilitated communication. Mental Retardation. 34(4) 231-242.

Donnellan, A. M., & Leary, M. R. (1995). Movement differences and diversity in autism/mental retardation. Madison, WI: DRI Press.

Dykens, E. M., Hodapp, R. M., & Leckman, J. F. (1994). Behavior and development in fragile X syndrome. Thousand Oaks, CA: Sage.

Gardner, H. (1983). Multiple intelligences. NY: Basic Books.

Hill, D. A, & Leary, M. R. (1993). Movement disturbance: A clue to hidden competencies in persons diagnosed with autism and other developmental disabilities. Madison, WI: DRI Press.

Horgan, J. (1995, November). Get smart, take a test: A long term rise in IQ scores baffles intelligence experts. Scientific American, 12-14.

Jacobson, J. W., Mulick, J. A., & Schwartz, A. A. (1995). A history of facilitated communication: Science, pseudoscience, and antiscience. American Psychologist, 50(9) 750-765.

Leary, M. R., & Hill, D. A. (1996). Moving on: Autism and movement disturbance. Mental Retardation, 34(1), 39-53.

Sheehan, C. M., & Matuozzi, R. T. (1996). An investigation of the validity of facilitated communication through the disclosure of unknown information. Mental Retardation, 34(2), 94-107.

Thelen, E. (1995). Motor development: A new synthesis. American Psychologist, 50(2) 79-95.

Weiss, M. J. S., Wagner, S. H., & Bauman, M. L. (1996). A case of validated facilitated communication. Mental Retardation 34(4) 220-230.

Weiss, M. J. S., & Zelazo, P. R. (Eds.) (1991). Infant attention: Biological constraints and the influence of experience. Norwood, NJ: Ablex Publishing.

Williams, D. (1994). Somebody somewhere. NY: Times Books.

Anne M. Donnellan, PhD, is a Professor in the School of Education at the University of Wisconsin–Madison. A long time member of the professional advisory panel of the Autism Society of America, she is known internationally for her numerous books and articles which include co-authoring the books *Movement Differences and Diversity in Autism/Mental Retardation, Alternatives to Punishment*, and *Progress without Punishment,* and co-editing *The Handbook of Autism,* and her training, research, and advocacy work on behalf of children and adults with significant communication and behavior challenges.

Paid For The Privilege

The theme of *Paid for the Privilege* is quite simple. It is an account of a marketing director's experiences in a day center for disabled adults where he had been hired to find work for people whose lives are segregated from the social and economic mainstream.

But, more importantly, it is an account of a series of transformations that occurred in this community. Their introduction to communication techniques gave voices to people who had grown up without speech and been labeled mentally retarded.

Specifically, *Paid for the Privilege* is a sounding board for people who are unable to reveal their thoughts, needs, dreams and longings through conventional communication channels. Identified as "autistic," they are typically regarded as aloof, unaware, and withdrawn. The author discovers that none of these descriptions is true. Their stories tell of acute sensitivities, insight, and wisdom. He quickly learns that he has more to learn than to teach and in recording his own story lets the reader share in the privilege.

About the author:

Dan Reed has been Marketing Director at Midway Training Services (MTS) in St. Paul, Minnesota, since 1992, when he was hired to help people with disabilities find more independent and meaningful lives.

An active member of several city and state boards and committees, Dan works to bridge the gaps that separate disabled (labeled) people from mainstream academic, occupational and social opportunities. In 1995 his successes earned him the Minnesota Association of Special Needs Personnel Award for Outstanding Community Service.

Prior to joining MTS Dan co-owned a successful electronics applications business but was looking for something new, something completely different. At the same time MTS was looking for someone from the business world—someone completely different, with fresh ideas. His book is an account of the surprisingly different experiences that were in store for them all.